TO113435

Queen of Prophets

QUEEN of PROPHETS

The Gospel Message of Medjugorje

DUDLEY PLUNKETT

IMAGE BOOKS
DOUBLEDAY
NEW YORK LONDON TORONTO SYDNEY AUCKLAND

AN IMAGE BOOK
PUBLISHED BY DOUBLEDAY
a division of Bantam Doubleday Dell Publishing Group, Inc.
666 Fifth Avenue, New York, New York 10103

IMAGE and DOUBLEDAY are trademarks of Doubleday,
a division of Bantam Doubleday Dell Publishing Group, Inc.

First published in 1990 by Darton, Longman and Todd Ltd;
this Image edition published May 1992, by special arrangement
with Darton, Longman and Todd Ltd.

The scriptural quotations are taken from The Jerusalem Bible,
published and copyright © 1966, 1967, and 1968 by Darton, Longman
and Todd Ltd and Doubleday, a division of Bantam Doubleday
Dell Publishing Group, Inc., by permission of the publishers.

Library of Congress Cataloging-in-Publication Data
Plunkett, Dudley.
  Queen of prophets: the Gospel message of Medjugorje /
Dudley Plunkett.
      p.   cm.
  Originally published: London: Darton, Longman, and Todd, 1990.
  Includes bibliographical references.
  1. Mary, Blessed Virgin, Saint—Apparitions and miracles
—Yugoslavia—Medjugorje (Bosnia and Hercegovina) 2. Mary, Blessed
Virgin, Saint—Prophecies.   3. Catholic Church—Doctrines.
I. Title.
BT660.M44P58   1992   91-37709
232.91′7′0949742—dc20   CIP
ISBN 9780385421522

147687453

Contents

Acknowledgments

Very many people have contributed to this book. The testimony of some of them is recorded in its pages, and others have helped by their writings, their conversation, their friendly support and their prayers. I would like them to know how much I appreciate all they have done. However, I would especially like to thank Fr Svetozar Kraljevic and Heather Sterling, who read and commented so helpfully on the manuscript, and Fr Alan Griffiths who commented acutely on certain points. I am also grateful to Sarah Baird-Smith, my editor, for her helpfulness. I hope that I have done some justice to the wise advice I have received, but the responsibility for the final text must remain with me.

Introduction

The continuing apparitions of the Virgin Mary in the Croatian village of Medjugorje in Yugoslavia, which began in 1981, have attracted the attention of the media, tourists, theologians and more than ten million pilgrims. There are several books available in English in which the interested reader can find historical accounts and spiritual analyses of the Medjugorje events, especially those by Kraljevic, Laurentin, Faricy and Rooney, O'Carroll, and Craig, among others listed in the bibliography at the end of this book. However, there has not hitherto been any extended work that sets out to explore the spiritual significance and the implications for everyday life in secular western society of the hundreds of messages given by Mary over this period to a group of young Yugoslav villagers.

There are many different ways in which people have sought meaning and purpose in life which do not easily stand up to spiritual scrutiny. Old and New Testament promises of God, which are being proclaimed by prophets in modern times as much as they were in other eras, challenge the importance attached to material possessions, social and political status, rational-scientific thinking, and to personal pleasure and self-absorption. This book concerns one such prophetic message. Many believe that the Virgin Mary has come as a messenger from God in our time, to call people back to religious belief and to a willing co-operation in Jesus Christ's work of redemption through commitment to loving God and to living in peace.

I think it is important to acknowledge from the outset that I write from a standpoint of Christian belief, and that I accept the authenticity of the apparitions in Medjugorje. My hope in writing this book is to help make Mary's messages and their relevance more widely appreciated. Because of the spiritual nature of these matters, reason and evidence will not be sufficient to convey their truth and relevance. Belief in spiritual realities for the Christian does not imply rejecting reason and evidence, however, so much as going beyond them under the benevolent inspiration of the Holy Spirit. Christian spiritual reality can on the other hand be tested against a number of perspectives, the most essential being Scripture, church tradition, private revelation, the *sensus fidelium* (or inspiration of the Christian people), and, not least, the actual spiritual response of believers. These various perspectives are needed in a work about Medjugorje. They cannot be entirely separated from each other, but the early chapters of the book seek to focus attention upon each of them in turn.

There is, first of all, an indispensable scriptural foundation to any authentic prophecy. Mary's title of Queen of Prophets is an ancient one. A prophet speaks for God. Some may say that God does not need intermediaries, and that we need only to go straight to God in prayer. But, as chapter one will recall, there always have been prophets to point the way to God, from the earliest recorded times up to our day. Furthermore, most people today are not turning to God in prayer, and if there is one cardinal principle of Mary's Medjugorje messages it is the great need the whole of humanity has to find its way back to God. Secondly, Mary's intervention in Medjugorje is consistent with the role that Christian tradition in East and West has recognized her to have. In chapter two an attempt is made to summarize the main tenets of this tradition, particularly for the non-Catholic reader.

Chapter three is concerned with the content of the messages reported by the Medjugorje visionaries. Private revelations, such as those to mystics, saints and visionaries, have not introduced new dimensions to the Christian faith, but they can help in confirming its relevance to changing human circumstances.

There are two ways in which the authenticity of a spiritual

reality can be assessed, and these form the subject of chapter four. There is the spontaneous response of belief found in the people, who must often lead in matters of faith, even though church authority will eventually have to confirm or disconfirm their claims. And, following the adage that a good tree is known by its fruits, there are the observable results of the phenomenon, and thus in the case of Medjugorje there is a need to examine the way in which people who have been affected have altered their moral and spiritual behaviour.

The later chapters of the book look at the way in which the events and messages of Medjugorje are challenging the Church and secular society to grow spiritually and to open minds and hearts to the divine presence, so that God's creation can have its intended fulfilment both in this world and in the building of the heavenly kingdom.

Despite the disregard for Marian apparitions and indeed for religious phenomena in general in modern society, there are many signs of a revival of interest in spiritual matters as people search far and wide and increasingly intensely, for a meaning or a truth on which they can base their lives. Many who have had a personal experience of Medjugorje, as I have done, are convinced that no such seeker, and certainly no Christian, should ignore what has been happening there. Can the wider Christian Church come to accept that the apparitions, the messages, and all the extraordinary manifestations of spiritual vitality in Medjugorje over the past eight years, are the way that Mary is being used by God to bring about a worldwide change of heart?

1

Prophecy and God's Purposes

The prophet as messenger and interpreter

The prophet is one who speaks for God. The role is given not as a privilege for a faithful worshipper but as a channel for a message of vital significance. There is a note of urgency that is characteristic of prophecy. This is not to say that all prophecy has to do with the end times, or that this book is imbued with that view. It is simply that God can make known the truth about the spiritual state and destiny of his people by charging an individual to speak it out. In Catholic tradition the Virgin Mary and many of the saints are regarded as mystical or visionary figures who served God in prophetic roles, whether in their lifetimes on earth or thereafter.

Who are the prophets, and are there any alive today? In biblical times prophets appeared with relative frequency, from the time of Moses to that of Jesus Christ himself, who was both a prophet and the Messiah, giving and fulfilling prophecy. Looking back, we can accept these prophets as messengers of God because we have seen evidence that their prophecies came to pass. But would we have believed the man 'crying in the wilderness' in AD 30? To open our minds and make them receptive to present-day prophecy we should perhaps ask ourselves this question. A group I was in recently was discussing whether there were any living prophets. One woman was quite adamant. No, there were no prophets today. She had never seen or heard of one. This amazed other members of the group, who began to enumerate their own prophets: Mother Teresa, Archbishop Tutu, Clifford Hill,

1

Pope John Paul II. The ensuing discussion was a lively one, because the group was thrown back onto its assumptions about prophets and prophecy. Did prophets need to be unusual figures speaking in strange ways? Did prophets only address particular groups of people who were already 'in the know', or were they part of everyday life? Could there be a place for the special knowledge of prophets and prophecy in a scientific world, one in which things are regarded as believable according to the reasonable or tangible evidence for them? Is the whole matter of prophets worth talking about? Do we need them?

Prophets are guides for the spiritual journey, a journey we all have to make: those who have always believed, those who have been converted, those who feel they are agnostics, and even those who have rejected belief in God. We are all spiritual pilgrims because we all long for an explanation for our existence. We want our being to have some significance, but we have to look to someone or somewhere else for this. It may be to our families, our friends, or our colleagues. It may be to the evidence we have that whatever we are doing is affecting the outside world in some way. Or it may be that we look to God for our meaning and purpose. The prophets were always those who kept their eyes on the distant horizon, not necessarily to foretell the future, but rather to provide a map for the traveller.

There were many prophets in the Bible who did not get a hearing in their time, and the same must be true today. If there are prophets in our contemporary world, how would we recognize them, and what would they be talking about? Usually prophets seem to have been people who interpreted visible signs of the times rather than spoke from an entirely different perspective. In other words, they began from where things were, even if they saw them so differently from everyone else that their messages were often misunderstood or ignored.

Today, if we seek to read the signs of the times, we are bewildered for choice of perspective. We can adopt a purely materialistic view, and look at social and economic trends, extrapolating them to anticipate the future. Forecasting, of either the weather or the economy, resembles this, but it falls short of prophecy. Or we can take a more philosophical stance and reflect upon our nature and our needs, and understand the evolution of events within a rationalist framework. But then we only deal with what is already given; there is no element of special knowledge of what is to come. We can also turn to a variety of messages from mystical sources, such as spiritualist mediums or gurus. Or indeed we can follow the Judaeo-Christian tradition of prophets who announce themselves as messengers of God, and who, to be regarded as authentic or for their writings to be a part of the canon of Scripture, have had to be endorsed by the believing community.

The prophecies of the Virgin Mary in Medjugorje have as their specific purpose to urge us to change our lives spiritually and to help those around us to do likewise. There is an immediacy about them, since they warn that we should not postpone our conversion. This echoes Scripture, which is full of stories about people who got the message too late, like the five foolish virgins who allowed their lamps to go out (Matthew 25), or about those who grew tired waiting: 'Days go by and visions fade' (Ezekiel 12:22). 'When that day comes', will we be ready, are we expecting it, are we already on the watch, or do we allow days to go by when we actually forget that we are mortal, that we are accountable to one who is a God of justice as well as of mercy? We are urged to believe that the Lord is going to accomplish his will in his own time, indeed in our time. Reading the spiritual signs of our times demands of us both attentiveness and response; it is an everyday concern. And, although their tone is always gentle and loving, the messages of Medjugorje confront us continually with just this concern.

Prophecy in biblical times

The truth believed by Jews and Christians to inhere in the Scriptures rarely presents itself in the form of a literal or propositional truth, like science or good journalism. It is more akin to a symbolic or poetic truth, though this understates the reality. We read the Scriptures to meditate upon the word of God, to let it inform us and change us. The word of God is both signified and signifier, it is *the* truth expressing itself. Since Scripture concerns itself with the relationship between humanity and the Creator, it is essentially prophetic. Scripture describes a process, but not chronologically: we are both within and at different stages of a process. Scripture therefore helps us to understand the unfolding future as well as the present and the past.

Although the Trinity is not explicitly revealed in the Old Testament, Christians find its texts filled with prophetic references to the life and teachings of Jesus as Messiah and to the action of the Holy Spirit. For example, Psalm 24 is prophetic in the sense that it makes clear the distance between the sovereign God and ourselves, and yet gives us the consolation of the knowledge that God can be approached by him 'whose hands are clean, whose heart is pure'. This figure of innocence is the type of Christ, the one 'who has the right to climb the mountain of Yahweh', and 'to stand in his holy place'. How can people enter God's presence? Only through the work of redemption, the knowledge of God with which the Holy Spirit fills their hearts, the innocence restored to them. In this psalm, the Holy Spirit is the fullness of the earth, that is, its fruitfulness. He is mercy from God. He is longing for God. He is the confidence of the people that the King will come, and he is with those who swing back the doors to 'let the King of glory in'.

This psalm presents the key questions with which this book is concerned. Have we understood how great the Lord is, how far he is from us in his thoughts, intentions, powers and virtues? Can we encapsulate God by our thoughts? Can we even think of him, measure the Absolute, contain the Infinite, comprehend the Holy? We are reduced to total silence, nothingness, in his presence. And, to crown it all, we have sinned. We have turned from him, inflated ourselves in our own imaginations to the point of showing contempt for God, so that we would be completely without recourse if a plan of redemption had not been made.

If Jesus the Messiah had not been conceived by the Holy Spirit of the Virgin Mary, it would mean that the Father was leaving us in our darkness and sin. But he did send his only Son. He did send a light into the world to illuminate our hearts and to call us back to him. The Father of all sends us his Son, born of woman, but conceived by the principle of love, the Holy Spirit. If Mary is *the* immaculate conception, as Maximilien Kolbe pointed out, then the Holy Spirit is *the* life, the light, the love, that is, *the* practical source of our understanding of what is, and of our being able to come out of our darkness, sin and nothingness to respond to God's word. The word is given to us by the Holy Spirit, either through Scripture or directly by inspiration. For most Christians the starting point of their recognition of the action of the Holy Spirit is in their understanding of words of Scripture reaching their fulfilment.

'He has spoken by the prophets.' It is the Holy Spirit who passes on the messages of life. If a man speaks of God, it is the Holy Spirit who speaks in him. If a prophet speaks for God, it is the Holy Spirit who gives him utterance. If Mary speaks to us of God, it is the Holy Spirit who is speaking in her. He, the spouse of Mary, united to her as the bride, the Church, the people of God, is the one who brings the Word of God to her, and makes her fruitful.

The psalms so often need to be read as referring to Jesus, and from our vantage point beyond the historical life of Christ we can use them as a constant source of inspiration and affirmation. We can see their prophetic dimensions. Thus, if we read Psalm 109:4–5 as about any just man, it shows a nobility of soul, but the rest of the psalm might seem to dwell upon the punishment of the guilty: 'In return for my friendship they denounce me, though all I had done was pray for them; they pay me back evil for kindness and hatred for friendship.' Seen as a prophecy referring to Jesus, however, it is clear that the psalm is about the mercy and justice of God, always in tension. God wants to deal with us with mercy, but he cannot while we remain proud and unrepentant. He pours out his mercy most particularly on those who are helpless, friendless, abused, or anguished, and who cry out to him. This is the terrible story of Jesus: no one loved so much; no one was so rejected, so unloved, so unknown. And all the time he prayed for his accusers and executioners. He was the victim of a conspiracy of hatred, of unprovoked attack (v. 3). 'I have become an object of derision, people shake their heads at me in scorn' (v. 25).

The psalm suggests the suffering of Jesus as one who had to endure human evil not merely as physical assault but as a plunging into a deep moral chasm. He suffered in his soul as much as in his body. His sensitivity to what was lacking in integrity and love was so great that the presence of evil could cause him pain in a way that we are not able to understand. The final note of the psalm, however, is one of joyful thanks and praise, and of confidence that God stands especially with the friendless and brings redress to the innocent. We cannot hope to encompass these truths unless we read such passages invoking the Holy Spirit to guide our understanding, to help us go deeper into Christ's love and nobility of soul, and thus to recognize the work of redemption that is foreshadowed.

The Exodus as prophecy

Perhaps the simplest way to appreciate the importance of the prophetic dimension of Scripture is to concentrate on particularly relevant examples from the Old Testament and from the New. The story of the Exodus of the Israelites from Egypt and their arrival in the promised land is still a source of insights into the action of God in our present world. Frances Hogan makes the most puzzling texts come alive with the reflections she gives us (Hogan, 1984). Egypt is not only the country where the Hebrews are enslaved; it is also the scene of their own slavery to sin. Their liberation is not merely social and political, but spiritual, and in fact *primarily* spiritual because from this time forward they are a people bound by a covenant to God. Thus, the Exodus can be taken as an allegory for all times, telling the story of humanity's journey away from oppressive evil and sinfulness towards a new existence in freedom and justice, in response to a divine calling.

Applied to our time, the Exodus story helps to reveal that we are of an age that is tragically confused about its journey, lacking a sense of meaning and direction for life. Like the Hebrews in Egypt, we have grown accustomed to the state in which we live. We are likely to protest if anyone asks us to make any substantial change. In fact it hardly seems an exaggeration to say that our captivity, in our present-day Egypt, is self-willed. The point is not to find a target for blame, since we are all bearers of responsibility for problems of slavery and repression, or in modern terms hunger, disease, injustice, poverty and conflict, but rather to see from where change might come. My understanding of the spiritual meaning of Exodus, as indeed of Medjugorje, is that we are not being condemned but we are being asked to change. And we are being reassured that profound change is possible. It comes, however, from God, not from ourselves.

It cannot be said that the modern world has no place for a god, for it has only too many gods. The problem is that it devotes itself scrupulously, even religiously, to the service of gods which are idols. It is not too strong a characterization of our world to say that it is idolatrous because it behaves exactly like the ancient Hebrews who, when they lost hope, fashioned their own gods out of precious metals, and worshipped them. Is it not the case that our world worships gods made by human hands and minds: such as wealth, science, ideologies and cults, fashion, beauty, sex, fame and the like? In late-twentieth-century society, money is one of the main measures of worldliness. However spiritual we are, we continue to have material needs, but how high on our list of priorities do these come? Conversion to a God who is not an

7

idol may be the truth that has seemed too simple to be believable.

Pharaoh could not believe it. His heart was hardened, and of course this was his downfall, as it led him eventually into the disastrous pursuit across the Red Sea. Our Exodus could be the discovery of that God, just as the Hebrews found him at the Red Sea and on Mount Horeb. Pharaoh's hardness of heart might translate to our era as the claims of Christians being ignored in many parts of the world. War and injustice rage; innocence is betrayed. The powers live secure in their rejection of God. The faithful suffer oppression, ridicule and pain. The prophets warn that God cannot be mocked. The Lord gives signs, but the faithless cannot read them. One day the pattern will become clear, and even those who have made themselves blind and deaf will be obliged to see and to hear.

2

Prophecy Fulfilled

The human journey

In many ways surprisingly, it appears possible today, in what is so often regarded as a secular age, to detect a growing interest in biblical and other prophecies. Within a very brief span of years there has been a change of mood in the world. Humanity is experiencing a profound shifting of concerns, of aspirations, of expectations. This is distancing many from faith in the possibility of progress and growth through science, technology and rationality, or through the restructuring of societies through political designs and power-bloc diplomacy. There is a breakdown in the self-confidence of the nations emerging from the era of post-war materialism, and a deeper sense of what our future really depends upon is asserting itself. It is this deeper sense, of a more holistic and spiritual significance to the human journey, that I believe matches and responds to the religious dynamic of Medjugorje.

I am not assuming that the world at large is about to credit the prophetic messages of the Virgin Mary, at least not without direct divine inspiration, but all over the world people are searching for ways out of the intolerable evils that have humanity in their grip. What are these ways, and which should we follow? The Bible foreshadows our modern dilemmas, and its prophecies have relevance for our times. Among the pathways followed by the Hebrew people in their Exodus through the Sinai desert I see at least four which correspond to those being taken today by those who are seeking deliverance.

First, there is the negative response of pessimism, either through the abandoning of hope or the placing of hope in false directions or idols. When the Israelites felt thirst, and were tested, they at first rebelled in despair, but later their faith brought them water from the rockface, while the hard-hearted Egyptians suffered the plague of thirst with their rivers turned to blood (Wisdom 11). This thirst is still raging in the world, but it is not called by its name. We find no rest until we find rest in God, but we deny this and live as if we could be independent of the Creator. We satisfy our thirst with substitutes: knowledge, pleasure, power, sensations of the body, narcotics, alcohol, relationships of any kind, drugs, social and political theories, sleep, food, obsessions, neuroses, attacks, wars, self-delusions, collective myths, dropping out, tuning out, forgetting. As Christians we can now see, as the Israelites did, that we have thirsted in order to be tested and to learn what it is that the pagans suffer. We live in a pagan world, afire with thirst but unable to find the remedy.

Second, there is the way of submission or endurance in the desert, and the stoical facing of every suffering before any hope can be acknowledged. Surely large sections of humanity today are in the desert. The great masses who suffer from hunger and oppression in Africa, Asia and Latin America, the prisoners of conscience, dissenters in asylums, the physically and mentally ill or handicapped, those enduring incurable or painful diseases, so many of these must wonder whether they have been abandoned, or what is the meaning and purpose of what they are obliged to bear. How do some such people resist? How are some of them even strong enough to help others? Has suffering a meaning? Can it purify? Moses tells the people: 'Have no fear. Stand firm, and you will see what Yahweh will do to save you today . . . Yahweh will do the fighting for you: you have only to keep still' (Exodus 14:13–14). It was when the Hebrews saw the miracle of the Red Sea that they learned to fear the Lord and were able to put their trust in him and in his prophet, Moses. Must those who suffer await consolation or must they be roused to protest? Either way, the desert experience may have a vital, if mysterious, part to play in the Exodus in our modern world.

Third, there is the personal pathway of conversion to a search for value and meaning, in response to a call and a promise. God dealt directly with the leaders of the Israelites. They were aware of his majesty as the mountain was veiled in cloud. The people agreed to live by the covenant: 'We will observe all the commands that Yahweh has decreed' (Exodus 24:3, 7), and Moses sprinkled them with the blood of the sacrifice, saying (v. 8), 'This is the blood of the covenant that Yahweh has made with you, containing all these rules'. This seals the work of Exodus, the saving of the people and the setting up of the new relationship between God and his people. It also anticipates prophetically the Last Supper and the new covenant. The stature of Moses is unparalleled, as he is singled out by God for these august tasks. The Lord gives extensive messages of guidance to Moses, which are recorded in chapters 24–31 of the Book of Exodus. It is sobering to remember that during the forty-day period when the Lord was giving his message to Moses on the mountain, the Israelites were fashioning the golden calf to worship. Is the same not happening today as the messages of God through the Blessed Virgin Mary can hardly penetrate a distracted and worldly culture, even of those who claim to be believers? It is not a question of reading the messages, but of responding in faith to their prophecy of divine love and their call to complete abandonment to God.

And, fourthly, there is the encountering of value and meaning in the world, and especially in other people, so that the journey across the desert is finally made possible by its being shared with a united and peaceful community. The Hebrews were not freed from Egypt simply to roam the world for their own satisfaction. It was part of their service to God to live within his covenant and to go to the promised land, giving him praise and glory. So, true Christians today do not take their faith for granted, but live it ever more intensely so that it produces fruit for the greater glory of God. The pathway of conversion follows a thread provided by Providence, though this journey is not always overtly religious. There are those who discover grounds for hope in a specific faith, but others come to a turning point in their lives only after experience of tragedy, loneliness or fear of meaninglessness.

The way we live will reflect our faith, and thus those who seek God are unlikely to be true to their search if they are not at the same time concerned with the good of their neighbours and of the rest of humanity. For this reason, the Exodus must eventually take us through the territory of other people, family, community, those with power and without, friends and enemies. It cannot be that our journey is to involve an inward-looking search for individual completeness. It must be to share, in every sense, the labour and blessings of our lives and times. The building of humanity must be part of the journey. Because we are fragmented in our societies and groupings or, worse still, in our individuality, one of the inescapable tasks of our existence must be to create humanity, to humanize ourselves as a single family, to become a people, just as the Hebrews did, if we are to be led by the Lord through and out of the desert (Exodus 13:22).

The song Moses gave to his people, after having sight of the promised land and blessing the twelve tribes just before his death on Mount Nebo, was one of warning about how they should live to enjoy the Lord's favour, and what would be the response of the Lord if they worshipped alien gods (Deuteronomy 32–34). He saw how they would grow fat in Canaan, become complacent and look for something new. They would rebel. But the Lord would always care for them like an eagle looking after her young, bearing them on her wings. The test for them was to remain faithful so as to enjoy the land, and this meant holding fast to the Law, carrying it out faithfully, and handing it on to their children.

Prophecy in the gospel tradition

The principal prophetic figure of the New Testament is Jesus himself, as innumerable references illustrate, most often by

12

making connections between the Old Testament and the New. The prophecy of Isaiah of the springtime of deliverance (Isaiah 61) is surely one of the clearest prophecies in the Bible. This is because Jesus took it up directly in the synagogue at Nazareth and made the extraordinary claim: 'This text is being fulfilled today even as you listen' (Luke 4:21). In this case, Isaiah has a vision which does effectively illuminate the beginning of Jesus' public ministry, but it also bears upon our present, because the remainder of the chapter speaks of the rebuilding of what has lain desolate: 'They will rebuild the ancient ruins, they will raise what has long lain waste, thcy will restore the ruined cities, all that has lain waste for ages past' (v. 4). And later in the chapter the prophet speaks of the 'cloak of integrity' and how the Lord will 'make both integrity and praise spring up in the sight of the nations' (vv. 10–11). We do not know how these words apply to our time, but they are promises that remain valid, and it is not too difficult to see their effect in the world and in the Church. We have only to think of such events as the interdenominational charismatic renewal, as well as Medjugorje itself, though these are only signs of the greater springtime which takes place in individuals' hearts and in the coming of the kingdom of heaven.

On many occasions Jesus draws attention to prophecies being fulfilled. At the Last Supper he anticipates the moment when David's prophecy, 'The man who shared my bread has lifted his heel to trip me up', is to come true (John 13:18–19), and on the road to Emmaus he gives the lesson in interpretation of prophecy that makes the hearts of his two companions burn within them (Luke 24:32). We can understand such prophecy only by recognizing that God exists outside of time and space. The passage of time is not a constraint upon God, and therefore a prophecy is like a glimpse of God's perspective on reality as he surveys the past, the present and the future in procession before him. This means that he does not always speak through his messengers to foretell the future, but any vision God grants is something eternal. It belongs to past, present and future and may reveal something that is eternally true, or which uses the past to illuminate the present or the future. The Sermon on the Mount is a prophetic teaching that is not future-oriented, but is eternal. It is the great message offered to us by Jesus from the Father, when he tells us what the Father has told him to say. This is therefore *the* prophetic statement of the gospel.

The one who magnifies the Lord

The New Testament reports only 124 words (in the Latin Vulgate) spoken by the Virgin Mary, more than two thirds of them in the prayer known as the Magnificat. In this prayer, spoken in the presence of her cousin Elizabeth, Mary proclaims the glory of God. She turns away from earthly things and gives her heart, that is, her whole being, to the Lord. Her joy is in the Lord; her heart is true, her hunger for God is assuaged. She finds that the Lord keeps his promises because she has understood what these promises are, and her prayer helps us to understand them. It is a narrowing of her meaning to see the Magnificat as a worldly proclamation, because it is full of the awareness of the living God, the God who lives in eternity. Moses was the person who had the vision of the first passover, the saving of the Hebrews; and it is Mary who best understands the new passover, the work of redemption. Pope John Paul II recalls her title, Mother of the Redeemer, in his encyclical letter of that name, because he wants to draw attention to her role, and to her consciousness of her role (Pope John Paul II, 1987). This consciousness is prophetically reflected in the Magnificat by references to the two passovers, at the Exodus from Egypt and at the redemption to be effected by Jesus, and to the connection between them. The Virgin Mary proves herself the prophet who knows the ways of the Lord, not out of her natural understanding, but because she is the chosen servant.

Mary's title as prophet does not originate with Medjugorje. It comes from the gospel, as Irenaeus pointed out in commenting on the Magnificat, when he speaks of her as 'prophesying for the Church' (Addis and Arnold, 1954: 539). Similarly, Pope John Paul says that the Magnificat 'ceaselessly re-echoes in the heart of the Church down the centuries', and comments that, 'by means of this truth about God the Church desires to shed light upon the difficult and sometimes tangled paths of man's earthly existence' (Pope John Paul II, 1987, pt. 3). Although he does not use the word prophet to describe her, Pope John Paul makes it clear that he sees Mary as speaking directly to our times on God's behalf.

Divine intervention in our times?

Many who believe in God do not look for divine intervention in the world, either because God is seen as beyond time and space, beyond sense experience, or because any such intervention is seen to imply that God's work was inadequate in its original conception. However, the mystical traditions of the world's religions, the myths about divine intervention, the life of Jesus Christ as well as of other figures who have been identified as divine messengers, and the belief in miracles, apparitions, and messages, such as those of Medjugorje, are as real for many as the world we live in day by day. These instances surely justify reflecting upon the situation of the world today and imply the possibility of faith in a God who can change things in accordance with a destiny that lies beyond us now, but to which we are invited if we make the effort of will to open our minds and hearts to the Spirit of God speaking through events and signs of our times.

The Bible is full of sudden and unexpected happenings that we call miracles, and which are seen as the acts of intervention, or signs of the presence and power of the unseen God. What are these signs for? They tell us that God cares for us, that he is never far from those who trust absolutely in him. The demands made on our faith and our lives by the messages of Medjugorje, when viewed from a secular perspective, are no different from the demands of the Sermon on the

Mount or from what we see being lived in the Gospels. For example, the life of St Joseph provides a perfect scriptural illustration of the mysterious interventionary power and inexorable demands of the divine word. The first two chapters of Matthew's Gospel relate the story of Joseph living through the most momentous events of his life. In each of a series of four dreams containing messages, he responds immediately in obedience to them as coming from God. Joseph does not take initiatives; instead he is wholly attentive to God's word. When something is demanded of him it comes suddenly as a word of command, and he humbly complies. His life is being . lived in a mystical dimension, even though he appears simply to be acting as a good father, loving and caring for his family.

These qualities of love, humility, attentiveness and obedience can be seen as not merely laudable in Joseph, but as exemplary for Christians of all times. St Joseph gives a living example of how love is at the source of God's word and of his own response to it. It is the energy that forges links to God, and forms all inner dispositions. Humility is seen in his willingness to be the instrument of God's purposes without needing to understand. It is the desire to concentrate on God rather than upon self. Attentiveness is evident in his attitude of recollection, of calm, of alertness to the Lord, and in his recognition of his signs and words. And obedience is shown by his self-abandonment to the will and plan of God. Prophecy would have no purpose if we were unable to respond to its message. Mary both tells us how to respond, and encourages those who do so. Indeed, each of her messages to the parish of Medjugorje ends with the significant phrase: 'Thank you for having responded to my call.'

Most religions have a story of divine intervention to explain their very existence. Many have holy books recording the original message received. In the case of Christianity, the birth of Jesus as God and man is the most significant event since the creation of humanity, and indeed as a kind of second creation because it inaugurates a new history culminating in eternal salvation. The gospel is the corpus of messages left by Christ, and contains all the knowledge of the spiritual domain necessary for salvation. Any further prophecies are necessarily consistent with the gospel, or they cannot be regarded as Christian.

It would be wrong, however, to disregard God's work, which continues today as in the Bible: 'He answers me and frees me from all my fears. Every face turned to him grows brighter and is never ashamed' (Psalm 34:4–5). People who have not believed in God need to be reassured that they are in his constant care. Words of Scripture and the messages and teachings of the Blessed Virgin Mary can bring this reassurance, a sense of the graciousness of God, a trust in his dealings with us, and an encouragement to the disheartened to turn to him for help. Prayer, Mary reminds us, is the hidden force that invites the power of God into the world. Those who think that God cannot or will not intervene in our world have ignored prayer. The prophecies of Medjugorje constantly affirm this. The main theme of Mary's messages is that prayer is essential to the spiritual life and to the fulfilment of God's plans, that God comes to us in prayer, and answers our prayers.

3

The Virgin Mary in Salvation History

The first prophecies to be found in the Bible are those spoken in the Garden of Eden to the serpent, and to Adam and Eve. The very first concerns the enmity to be established between the serpent, or the devil, and the woman, 'your offspring and her offspring' (Genesis 3:15). This prophecy has been taken by the early church fathers as a reference to the incarnation (Brown, 1978: 280; O'Carroll, 1986: 93; *Lumen Gentium*, para. 55). There is a Catholic tradition, which was reaffirmed by the Second Vatican Council but which is contested by other contemporary scholars, that there is a foreshadowing here of the Blessed Virgin Mary, whose offspring will oppose evil, while she will unite herself in an unparalleled way to Jesus in his combat, and thus fulfil a unique role in the work of human salvation (*Lumen Gentium*, para. 56).

The end of the Bible is seen, in this interpretation, to contain a sequel to the first prophecy in the victory of Jesus, the newborn child who is saved from the dragon, and the exaltation of his mother who, as the mother of God and a figure of the Church, is protected from, and withstands Satan (Revelation 12). Mary's place in God's plan of redemption is thus understood to be prophesied at the beginning and at the end of the Bible, as well as in the gospel accounts of the life of Jesus. The burden of these prophecies is to identify Mary as the created being who most closely shared the struggle waged by the Redeemer against the powers of evil. In Catholic tradition, this role of Mary's is not to be understood as in any way substituting for the redemptive work of Jesus, but simply reflects God's will to associate her with his Son's redemptive mission. The role of Mary thus counterbalances, and corrects, the role of Eve (Brown, 1978: 255). Eve was the first to transgress, and to bring about the fall. Mary, the new Eve, comes to bring Jesus the Saviour, and thus helps to restore what had been lost (*Lumen Gentium*, para. 56).

An interpretation which might otherwise be set aside as merely speculative takes on a totally different hue as Christians from different traditions acknowledge the significance of Mary's role through events occurring in our times. She is seen not only to be a prophetic figure or image in the Bible, but a prophet in her own right, both acclaiming God's mercy in the Magnificat, and in calling out to mankind to return to God in repentance, as she is believed by millions to have done at Lourdes and at Fatima, and now at Medjugorje. To be fully comprehended, these Marian apparitions must be placed alongside the background provided by the beliefs and practices of the Church through the ages, and particularly of the Catholic Church. Some brief account of this tradition is therefore essential if a theological dimension is to be discerned in the events of Medjugorje.

The Mother of God

The Catholic and Orthodox traditions are those that have especially honoured Mary. Both recognize her divine and her universal motherhood, her virginity, her sinlessness, and her sufferings shared with the crucified Saviour. Similarly, both proclaim her bodily assumption into paradise when, just as she had once drawn God's Son into her womb by her perfection and humility, so she was drawn back to him in his glory. These beliefs are questioned, and even rejected, by other Christian traditions, the main objection being that the cult of Mary is not scriptural. But is this valid? Mary's own words have been preserved in Luke's Gospel where she says, 'from this day forward all generations will call me blessed' (Luke 1:48). Has this prophecy not been left out of account by some in their consideration of Mary's role in the divine plan for our salvation?

The incontrovertible starting point in any reconciliation of these views must be to recognize Mary as the mother of the Redeemer. That the Gospels speak very little of Mary is no reason for us to neglect the part that she played. The one who 'bore the Son of the eternal Father' was undoubtedly being given a role of major importance. The incarnation is the measure of the degree to which God cared for his human creation. It was the highest point of humanity's destiny on earth to receive the birth of the Son of God. We were not only being redeemed; we were being accepted into a relationship that exalted us far beyond any conceivable purely material value of our lives. This is the great dawning for humanity and the fulfilment of the ancient promise of a saviour. That is why the angels sing, and why there are epiphanies for the shepherds and the kings. We cannot understand how great this event is, even though we follow the gospel account and take in the scene as it has been presented by artists and by the teaching of the Church. We cannot be more than dimly aware of the difference it makes to us that this child has been born, but is it not certain that Mary must have been granted a greater awareness of the miracle of that birth than any other human being in creation?

Awaiting the birth of Jesus, however, Mary gives voice to humility, not to pride or satisfaction: 'I am the handmaid of the Lord' (Luke 1:38). There is dignity, but no pride, as in the words of the Magnificat. Mary places all that she is at the service of the Lord. The role of handmaid of the Lord is a humble one because it leaves the initiative entirely with him. While this may seem acceptable in the light of faith, it contrasts with what usually happens in our everyday world that continually asserts its independence of God. Mary shows us that invoking God's will is not to abandon our dignity as persons but rather to enhance it by recognizing our relationship to the source of life. Through Mary we see that God's favour is above all associated with our humility and spiritual poverty. This is the message of the Magnificat and of the incarnation. It is also the truth reflected in the whole of Mary's life, veiled as it is in the gospels out of her very humility.

A model of faith

The God-bearing act of Mary, and the fact that she accompanied Jesus from the beginning to the end of his life, standing by his cross as he endured his agony when nearly everyone else had fled, suggests her to us as the model of Christian faith (*Lumen Gentium*, para. 53). She cannot have known in any factual way who her son was; she could only have known by faith. But she was ready to accept this mystery, and to accept it to such a degree that the Word was able to take flesh in her. Mary's words in reply to the angel Gabriel, 'Let what you have said be done to me' (Luke 1:38), imply a profound preparation and self-emptying in order that God's will could be absolutely respected and welcomed. And her anxiety when the boy Jesus is lost for three days shows us that she was not given divine foreknowledge of what was to happen.

Mary must have lived in faith from the time of Jesus' conception, all through his hidden life, and up to his death and her own. Mary experiences the fateful passover as the companion and witness to her son. No words of hers are recorded from this time in the gospels – surely an acknowledgement that her suffering was within. The focus is upon Jesus, while she accepts the humble yet sublime status of the faithful mother, at hand always, suffering with her son, giving him comfort and strength, if only to support him in making his final act of obedience to death on the cross. Mary is the witness of this death, the silent one who sees and understands what is happening, while the crowd jeers. Thus at the centre of the Calvary scene we can know the story of our redemption through the mind and heart of Mary. She does not need to change a word of her canticle before Elizabeth, even though it might seem that every word of the Magnificat had been

21

thwarted by the crucifixion. Mary cannot have *known* that Jesus would rise from the dead. She could only have faith, like every other Christian.

What we see in Mary, therefore, is how faith is nurtured in the human soul. We can sense the power of her faith from the very few details that the gospels give of her life. It was not necessary for her to say or do a great variety of things to give evidence of her faith. Faith and holiness are one, and her life conformed to the truth which she knew through faith. Her Magnificat prayer is a hymn of praise to God's love and mercy for those who accept him in faith: the poor, the House of Israel, the Church. This faith is renewed generation after generation, just as our faith in the incarnation is renewed with each repetition of Gabriel's words in the Hail Mary prayer.

Mary was human, not divine, and it is her faithfulness, not her powers, that we honour most in her. Therefore Catholics and non-Catholics will agree that we can have a direct relationship to the Father, the Son and the Holy Spirit without the need for intermediaries such as Mary and the saints. The only question is how God intends us to see Mary, and whether he has a special role for her in his plan for our salvation. Was she simply a kind of surrogate mother, used by God the Father to bring Jesus to birth as a man but without any enduring importance? Or did the Father intend to confer on humanity an honour that we could only comprehend through his allowing his divine Son to be born of a woman, who thus comes to represent all of humanity and serves also as the channel by which the graces of redemption reached us all through the incarnation? If it is the latter, as Catholic and Orthodox tradition holds, is perhaps this unique role not confirmed by the universal motherhood conferred upon Mary by Jesus from his cross when he gave her, literally all he had left in the world, to the apostle John? The Second Vatican Council thus felt able to refer to Mary as 'mother to us in the order of grace' (*Lumen Gentium*, para. 62) and also to recall the title of mediatrix which many church fathers, saints and popes have applied to her in view of her unique relationship to each of the members of the Blessed Trinity (*Lumen Gentium*, para. 62; but see also O'Carroll, 1986: 156). Mary is the daughter favoured and chosen by the Father, she is the mother of Jesus who remains united to the Son in his redemptive mission, and she is the spouse of the Holy Spirit, from whom she received the fruit of her womb, the incarnate saving power of God.

The *Theotokos*, the God-bearer, and not only Jesus, has become a 'sign of contradiction' at the present time. The mystery of the incarnation, of God's act in joining creation and the Divinity through Mary, is difficult to comprehend, as is the special distinction Mary was given by her second *fiat* at the cross, when she accepted the motherhood of all humanity. Her role, once given, is for all time. That is why the Catholic and Orthodox Churches also celebrate the assumption and coronation of the Virgin in heaven. They hold that her earthly mission ended with her assumption, but her heavenly mission continues; as mother of Jesus and of the Church, Mary brings a unique power of intercession to the peaceful gathering of the human family. Jesus wills us all to be one, calling us to repentance and faith, and Mary continually pleads with us and for us, humbly and graciously, as at Medjugorje, desiring to unite all her children for the sake of the son whose redemptive martyrdom she shared.

Although it might appear from modern theological discussion that Mary has become less important to the Church, her devotees, like the millions upon millions who have heard the call of the Virgin at Lourdes, Fatima and Medjugorje, take her as a sure sign, a guide and support in prayer, in faith and in all the works of reconciliation and encouragement that Christians undertake in following her son. Contemporary Christianity may be in danger of losing the delicacy of the humble, docile, trusting, caring and whole-hearted spirituality represented by Mary. Mary offers inspiration for our religious development, not because she has power that is separate from that of God, but precisely because she is so united to him that she can be a *model* to us, as the Second Vatican Council expresses it. Because she was constantly

23

close to Jesus in body or in spirit, from his conception to when he was laid in the tomb, Mary can bring us to a better understanding of his life and of how he understood his mission and his crucifixion. Indeed, since Mary was a witness to the incarnation, the crucifixion, and the founding of the Church, when the Holy Spirit came upon the apostles at Pentecost, she uniquely sees the divine purposes enshrined in the Church throughout its history.

Mother of the Church

The extent to which Mary's presence and intervention have been relied upon and called forth by prayer throughout the history of the Church is evident from the use of the Hail Mary, the angelus, the rosary, as well as from the many feast days with their special liturgies, the religious orders taking her as their patroness, the devotional practices associated with shrines and pilgrimages, and the entrustment to Mary of whole nations by bishops and popes. All are testimony to and a celebration of her divinely inspired role. Countless churches are dedicated to the Blessed Virgin Mary, often with the title 'Our Lady'. The cathedrals of Notre Dame of Paris and Chartres are among the best-known examples, and it is worthy of note that the latter contains some 150 windows, sculptures and statues of the Virgin. Alongside constitutional, liturgical and theological developments within the Catholic Church there has been a mystical and devotional development focusing upon the Virgin Mary. For believers, truths of faith have been confirmed through the ages by the intervention of the Holy Spirit, prophesying through the saints and conveying messages through their spiritual intuitions. Among such manifestations the apparitions of the Blessed Virgin throughout the history of the Catholic Church have been of outstanding significance.

This book's length does not allow for a detailed account of the many ways in which Mary has carried out this prophetic role in history, but Medjugorje is only one of the many miraculous interventions that God has granted her. It is for this reason that the people have been so quickly able to understand what was happening, and why they have led the official Church in coming to terms with the meaning of the apparitions in Yugoslavia. For those who find this line of argument difficult to accept, it is necessary to recall the immense crowds who flocked to the scene of major apparitions such as those in Guadalupe, Lourdes and Fatima, long before they were given recognition by the responsible bishops or by the Church officially.

The apparitions in Guadalupe in Mexico, in 1531, were responsible for a million conversions to Christianity a year for several years among the Indian population. As is well known, Lourdes and Fatima have likewise affected the lives of many millions who have gone as pilgrims to find spiritual or physical healing through their prayers and the intercession of the Blessed Virgin. But Medjugorje is now attracting more pilgrims annually than either Lourdes or Fatima. One of the main indications of the authenticity of a particular Marian apparition for believers lies in the link to be found with the messages associated with other apparitions. The messages reported from these major apparitions have constantly emphasized the love Mary has for all her children, and her desire that they should turn to God in prayer and penance. In her love, expressed in its purest form at the birth and death of her divine son, there is a great sign of hope for humanity. Her love seconds the redemptive love of the heart of Jesus. Thus the clearest explanation for Medjugorje, from the believer's point of view, is that Mary is making a further appeal to the people who have not sufficiently heeded her messages in the past.

Catholic tradition sees the Blessed Virgin as a figure of the Church. Her life was fulfilled by bringing Jesus to birth and nurturing him, and then by accompanying him in his sacrifice, and entering into his glory. In a comparable way the Church has to bring Jesus to spiritual birth in the world, nurture his life among the people, and then accompany him in any trials, until the triumph of salvation is accomplished.

25

Mary therefore represents the Church, reflecting what it is, and what its destiny is to be. As mother of the Redeemer, and thus of all who are brothers and sisters in Christ, she has come to be regarded by Catholics especially as mother of the Church. In her nurturing and teaching role she expresses God's will for the Church. She is therefore a prophet, one who speaks for God. Not only in her lifetime, but throughout the history of the Church, Mary has been appealed to by the people to help and guide them. And this she has done, repeatedly. The contention of this book is that not only can Mary be utterly relied upon to respond to the appeals of the Church, but that she is now taking the initiative in calling all people to conversion at a time when secular materialism seems almost to have succeeded in suffocating the Church. By recognizing the significance of the apparitions in Medjugorje, and how acute and urgent the messages of Mary are for the Church and for the secular world today, Christians of all persuasions will surely become more reconciled with each other as well as with God.

4

The Medjugorje Messages as Prophecy

Mary is both a prophetic figure and a prophet; she is the 'woman adorned with the sun' (Revelation 12:1) and the voice calling out to the human race to come back to God. A prophet cannot be understood in isolation from a setting or tradition, and in Mary's case the tradition of the Hebrew prophets illuminates her mission. Not only did her life in many ways fulfil prophecies of the Old Testament, especially those of Genesis and Isaiah, but, a prophet herself, she proclaims the reign of Jesus and calls people to repentance. It cannot have been a coincidence that her first apparition in Medjugorje was on 24 June, the feast-day of the Baptist, the first prophet of the New Testament.

Because as a prophet the Virgin Mary belongs to a tradition, what she says is best understood within that tradition. It is not obvious to somebody knowing nothing of the Bible just what the import of her messages is, though it may well be that an individual responds directly to them through a special grace as often seems to happen to pilgrims in Medjugorje. The most fruitful way to read the messages, therefore, is alongside the prayers of the Church, the psalms, the prophets, the gospels, all the texts that the Church uses to be reminded of what has been revealed of the nature and the promises of God. In her prophetic role, Mary confronts the modern idols of possession and rationalism and restates the gospel values of detachment and of faith in a transcendent reality, in a God not constrained by the pretensions of human reason. Her God is the God of the Hebrew prophets and of the evangelists.

Mary awaits the birth of Jesus in all of us. Her essential message is: the world needs Jesus Christ, the Word, the love of God. Since she has asked in Medjugorje to be known as the Queen of Peace, and since she has continually emphasized the spiritual aspects of peace, this can be taken as a central focus of her message. Fr Tomislav Vlasic, a Franciscan priest who was spiritual director to the visionaries in the early years, has conveyed in very clear terms the significance of the apparitions as leading to peace through Jesus: 'Through these apparitions, the truths of the sacred Scriptures have become real and tangible; the reality of heaven, purgatory and hell has been confirmed: the truth that Jesus is the way to peace has become conscious and real.'*

The sequence of events

Medjugorje itself is a collection of hamlets, with an original population of about 3,400 people. It is a remote village lying upon a plateau between ranges of mountains (the word Medjugorje means 'between the mountains'), in the Croatian region of Yugoslavia. This area has had a strong Catholic tradition, especially in resisting four centuries of Turkish occupation. The people of Medjugorje itself had given an indication of their faith in the more recent past by erecting a ten-metre-high stone cross on the mountain that towers above the village to celebrate the 1,900th anniversary of the crucifixion in 1933. The mountain is now known as Krizevac (hill of the cross), and has been a particular focus of religious devotion since the apparitions began. Although local people were accustomed to pray the rosary, there had been no special devotion to the Virgin Mary, known locally as *Gospa*, up to the time of the apparitions. However, a local artist had years before painted the Virgin as if appearing by the church. This painting now hangs at the back of the church and, together

* Introduction to Father Vlasic's letter of 15 August 1983, privately published in 1984 by the late Peter Batty.

with the cross on the mountain, has become one of the best-known symbols of Medjugorje.

The apparitions began on 24 June 1981, when the Virgin Mary appeared to a group of young people who were out walking near their homes in Bijakovici, one of the small hamlets that make up the village of Medjugorje. None of them dared approach the apparition, and it was not until some of them returned with friends the next day that they heard the Virgin speak. The six young people who, as a group, saw the Virgin on the second day, were those who then continued to receive daily apparitions. Four of them – Marija, Vicka, Ivan and Jakov – have seen the Virgin virtually daily, with occasional interruptions, since then up to the time of writing; while the two others – Mirjana and Ivanka – have seen the Virgin only once a year since their daily apparitions ended some years ago.

It is one of the most extraordinary features of the visions that they have continued for so long. This is without precedent for Marian apparitions, and has led some people to be sceptical for that reason alone. However, the opposite reaction is as plausible. How could deceit have gone undetected for so long, and what interest would anyone have in continuing to expose a hoax to discovery by so prolonging it? Indeed, the fact that the young people have in the meantime grown from childhood to adulthood is in itself evidence of the authenticity of the visions. What personality would be capable of sustaining a deceit from the age, in Jakov's case, of ten to eighteen – years of such change in the processes of human development?

The visionaries have impressed all who have come into contact with them by their normality, despite all the special attention they have received in recent years. They differ in personal characteristics, Vicka being more outgoing than the others, Mirjana more intelligent, Marija more recollected, Ivan with a more developed sense of humour, and so on. They are well known and popular among the young people in the area, and they have endured close questioning by police, local government officials, psychiatrists appointed by

29

the officials, and also by a host of theologians, doctors and curious pilgrims, without their sanity or integrity ever being put in doubt.

The apparitions have been recorded on video by dozens of amateur and professional cameramen as well as being witnessed by thousands of others. I myself watched five of the visionaries during two apparitions in January 1984, and I noted at the time:

When the apparition occurs, the visionaries kneel down rapidly and simultaneously, and there is a definite alteration in their appearance. Their eyes widen and their gaze intensifies, converging upon an area of the wall facing them. At times their lips move silently, giving the impression of a conversation in which they are sharing in turn. They never look away from the spot where their eyes are fixed or acknowledge any other event that might be going on around them. As the apparition ends they make the sign of the cross, stand up, and quickly resume a normal composure and respond to the people round them.

There can never have been apparitions claimed that have been so fully scrutinized as these. The visionaries, with the prior agreement of the Virgin, have submitted to weeks of close study, using video, electro-encephalograms and batteries of neurological and physiological tests applied during their ecstasies. But these have left medical and psychological experts without any plausible scientific explanations (Joyeux and Laurentin, 1987). Of course, this does not make it any easier for people to believe, if they have no religious faith, and it may be this that led Mary to say, when the young visionaries asked her if they should participate in the tests, that they were *unnecessary*.

Mary's messages

When I speak of messages from Medjugorje I have mainly in mind about 250 no more than paragraph-length statements recorded and made public by the young visionaries over the period since 25 June 1981, when the Virgin Mary first spoke to them. It is necessary to adopt a broadly chronological presentation because the messages are not random reflections but elements of a coherent spiritual programme. The language is simpler than almost any conventional published work of spirituality, which must tell us something. But gone are the times when sceptical people could easily dismiss the messages as bland or banal. Anyone who thinks about them, or better still prays about them, must recognize how well they convey gospel values, how powerfully they draw us towards God's love and blessing, and yet how gently they bring to mind the failings in our spiritual lives that need correction: our lack of faith, of trust, of love, our worldliness, our laziness, our desire for human respect and our lack of perseverance.

This short book will not suffice to comment on all the messages. The following account is intended as a guide to their thematic content. It cannot substitute for reading and meditating upon the actual messages, few of which are quoted in their entirety here.*

The public messages can be seen as belonging to three phases. The first of these was up to 1 March 1984, during which time the Virgin gave messages mainly to the visionaries themselves, while they passed them on in an *ad hoc* fashion to their local priests and to numerous inquirers. In the second phase, there was a weekly message given through Marija for the parish and pilgrims. This lasted until 8 January 1987. Since that time there have been monthly messages, which have continued to be given through Marija, with occasional supplementary messages, often given to Ivan, up to the time of writing.

---

* The text of the messages intended for the parish of Medjugorje and for the world is given, for the period up to mid-1988, in *Medjugorje: Messages of Life*, 1988 (see Bibliography). Several other books listed contain partial texts. More recent messages are given in the successive issues of the magazines listed in the Bibliography.

The first phase
Mary spoke of her mission towards the end of this first phase.
She said:

> I have come to tell the world that God is truth: he exists.
> In him is true good fortune and fullness of life. I have come
> here as the Queen of Peace to tell the world that peace is
> essential for the salvation of the world. In God is found
> true happiness, who is the source of peace. (16/6/1983)

This theme of peace emerged several times in the first few
days of the apparitions: 'Peace, peace, peace; be reconciled
with one another' (26/6/81).

One of the striking characteristics of the messages is that
they are clearly the words of a mother speaking to her children, not a world figure giving advice about principles for
living. The tone is set from the beginning. In the first conversation with the visionaries, on 25 June 1981, Mary told them:

> You must realize that the humble performance of your
> human and Christian duties is enough to make you worthy
> of heaven.

Later she said:

> If you want to be very happy, live a simple, humble life,
> pray a lot, and do not worry and fret over your problems
> – let them be settled by God. (date unknown)

Many of the early themes, such as prayer, fasting, peace,
reconciliation, the cross, and the need for the gifts of the Holy
Spirit, only gradually revealed their full importance as they
were reintroduced and developed in later messages.

The cross   One of the themes that develops through successive
messages is that of the cross. Medjugorje reveals the cross:
physically on Krizevac, as well as spiritually, it is a central
feature. Mary, who stood beneath the cross on Calvary, points
to it, and to her son hanging on it.

It is natural for me to pray at the foot of the cross. The

cross is the sign of salvation. My son suffered on the cross. He redeemed the world on the cross. Salvation comes from the cross. (January 1982)

Later, especially around the time of the Feast of the Triumph of the Cross, on 14 September, Mary refers several times to the cross: '. . . pray at the foot of the cross for peace' (6/9/84), and 'In these days ensure that the cross is the centre of your life. Pray especially before the cross, from which will come great graces' (12/9/85). The related theme of reconciliation is referred to frequently from the beginning. Reconciliation includes both personal and spiritual dimensions, that is, peace among people and peace with God through sacramental confession. Reconciliation with God restores even the greatest sinner to innocence. Mary said: 'Humanity must become reconciled with God and between themselves. To do this they must believe, pray, fast and confess their sins' (27/6/81).

The Holy Spirit On 21 October 1983, Mary spoke of our dependence on the Holy Spirit: 'It is important to pray that the Holy Spirit will come down. When you have that, you have everything.' At Pentecost the following year she said:

. . . pray for the outpouring of the Holy Spirit upon all of your families and your parish. Pray, and you shall not regret it. God will give you the gifts and you will glorify him for them until the end of your life. (2/6/84)

Some months later, she re-emphasized this:

The most important thing in the spiritual life is to ask for the gift of the Holy Spirit, and when the Holy Spirit comes there is calm. When that happens everything around you changes. (October 1984)

Later messages, especially around Pentecost 1985, continued to develop this theme of the need to rely upon the Holy Spirit.

The second phase

It was on 1 March 1984 that Mary invited the parishioners to read a passage from St Matthew's Gospel (Matthew 6:24–34) every Thursday. This is the passage that tells us that we cannot serve two masters, that we must trust God, and seek his kingdom first. This is, as it were, the summary of the Medjugorje messages, and its proclamation to the parish marks a new phase in the Blessed Virgin's messages. Instead of the scraps of information that the parishioners had been getting from the visionaries there is now to be a more deliberate spiritual programme. This would seem to be a response by Mary to the devotion that had grown up in the village and among pilgrims too. It is worth noting, however, that by March 1984 Mary had already laid the practical spiritual foundations for her work in Medjugorje.

The six young visionaries were being spiritually prepared for their tasks. Most of those communications in the apparitions that have not been published concerned the spiritual formation of the visionaries, presumably because of the tasks that they are being asked to perform in dealing with pilgrims now, and in whatever situation evolves in the future in Medjugorje.

The priests who would serve Medjugorje had been identified. Fr Tomislav Vlasic, and Fr Slavko Barbaric who succeeded him as spiritual director to the visionaries, had emerged as gifted preachers, and were about to begin the extraordinary series of sermons and meditations later published in the grey-blue-red-yellow book series (Vlasic and Barbaric, 1984 and 1985).

Two other inspired young people, who received inner 'locutions' – Jelena and Marijana – had begun to play a significant role in Mary's work.*

---

* Inner locutions do not involve an apparition, as with the six visionaries, but simply an explicit internal awareness of a message, which the young girls say is not like any human form of communication.

A young people's prayer group had been formed at Mary's request for a four-year phase of formation.

Vicka had recorded the account Mary had given her of her life, and was ready to make it public when she was permitted to by the Virgin.

At least one of the visionaries, Mirjana, had received the ten secrets that Mary wished to tell her. She also knew which was to be revealed first, and when. And a letter had been sent to the Pope giving him a direct account of the apparitions and of their significance for the Church and the world. The text of the letter (dated 2 December 1983, and reproduced in O'Carroll, 1986) summarized what the visionaries had been allowed to say about the secrets and about a century-long trial of the Church which was said to be nearing its end.

The earliest parish messages are about the main purposes of the apparitions, and the overwhelming need for humanity to turn towards Jesus. The first point was that God has a plan for the parish of Medjugorje. It is not without significance that this particular place has been chosen. This would not seem to be connected with the identity of the individual visionaries. They have continually expressed surprise that they should have been selected, and any explanation must rest with the special plan for Medjugorje which God has entrusted to Mary. She asks us to pray and work for the realization of his plan, and she often says that she needs our prayers and sacrifices. We cannot be saved unless we are willing, and our willingness is a corporate matter, in the sense that our individual willingness is important for the salvation of others, and we can help each other along the road to salvation. Of Mary's role we are told that Jesus wishes to give special graces through her, that she loves us all, even those who are far away from herself and her son, and that she wants everyone to pray more. She speaks, too, of her sadness over those who are being lost in sin.

Turning to Jesus   The need for humanity to turn towards Jesus emerges in the messages on conversion (8/3/84), on adoration of the Blessed Sacrament (15/3/84), on honouring the wounds of Jesus (22/3/84), on sacrifice (29/3/84), on venerating the heart of Jesus (5/4/84), and on prayer (19/4/84). The Sacred Heart is the disposition of Jesus' heart and mind as he offered himself on the cross. This is the Jesus that Mary is able to reveal to us because she witnessed his death at close hand. She knew his intentions. She was privileged to read in some measure the divine heart of Jesus. She saw his heart pierced, and was able to understand its significance: the power of Jesus extending beyond death, and the victory over death that was won by the cross.

Prayer and fasting   In the messages for the parish there are many different words used for prayer, such as *adoration, veneration, honouring, offering, sacrifice*, or *dedication*, and they are a feature of nearly every message. Prayer is seen as the way forward for every situation, because it is the way by which humanity can reach God. As time passes, the messages continue to place a major emphasis on prayer, but there are several that relate to fasting also. Fasting is linked to prayer. In fact a virtual 'spiritual rule' of Medjugorje emerges with the 14 August 1984 message about prayer, including the daily rosary, and strict fasting twice a week. In an early message Mary had said that 'the best fast is on bread and water'; then she urged the parish to 'fast strictly on Wednesdays and Fridays'. A little later she said: 'Today I urge you to begin your fasting with all your heart.'

Prayer is mentioned in most of the messages in subsequent weeks, including praying with the heart (20/9/84), 'for the conversion of sinners, because the world is in great sin' (special message to Jakov, 8/10/84), and also family prayer, reading the Bible to encourage prayer, and living the messages by rooting them in our hearts. In November 1984 the messages emphasize the graces being given to the people, and the need to pray to understand this. Not every family can pray all together, but those who can should do so, and they should begin to renew family prayer (1/11/84).

In the new year Mary tells us 'to open your hearts to God as the flowers of spring seek the sun' (31/1/85). She later suggests prayer 'with your hearts and not as a routine' (2/5/85). This emphasis on prayer of the heart is a development that continues. Mary calls for a spirit of abandonment, that is, prayer even in tiredness, sacrifice, through the opening of hearts to the Lord of all hearts: 'Prayer will be both joy and rest for you' (30/5/85); 'hear every call of God and answer with your life' (11/7/85). Much is being asked of the parishioners of Medjugorje, so many of whom have physically tiring work to accomplish. And then they are asked, 'to accept and love all who come to you' (6/6/85), and to pray 'at the beginning and end of every day' (3/7/86).

In a sequence of messages Mary tells us that we cannot receive graces if we do not pray (12/6/86). And grace will turn our suffering into joy (19/6/86). The cross can become a joy if we pray for the grace to accept it (11/9/86), and we are to offer sacrifices with a special reverence towards God (18/9/86). An important prayer message is that of 2 October: we must say to ourselves, 'Now it is time to pray; now nothing else is important; now for me no person is as important as God.' And then, in several successive messages during the following month: 'Pray constantly' (16/10/86), 'pray for peace' (23/10/86), 'pray daily for the souls in purgatory' (6/11/86), 'pray unceasingly', and 'pray with your whole heart' (13/11/86).

The seasons Many of Mary's messages relate closely to the liturgical season of the year, though it is clear that she sees particular times as more important. The most important are Easter, Christmas and Pentecost, but also certain major feasts such as the Triumph of the Cross and the Assumption. It would seem that in following these seasons Mary accepts to live partly in our time, so as to be able to guide us in our everyday lives.

The messages at Christmas are especially beautiful. One of the recurring themes is that of joy. Christmas is the 'day of joy' (messages of 6/12/84, 13/12/84 and 20/12/84); we are to be continually joyful, even when Satan attacks us. Preparation for Christmas is living the messages, loving everyone, and abandoning ourselves to Jesus. We are to pray 'out of love, not out of compulsion because of the cross you are carrying' (29/11/84). She says 'do something positive for Jesus Christ' (20/12/84), and that is to lay a flower by his crib on Christmas Day as a sign of abandonment to him. The following year she pursues her gentle insistence. The messages of the Christmas season emphasize the true meaning of Christmas, one of love for God and neighbour, a time to give glory and praise to Jesus:

> I call you to prepare yourselves for Christmas with penance, prayer and works of love. Do not worry yourselves too much about material things, or you will not be able to live the feast of Christmas. (5/12/85)

As a result of living Christmas according to Mary's messages, we should be purified and able to go forward with greater abandonment to God and to Mary. As Christmas approaches in 1986 Mary's messages have a special atmosphere of joy and expectancy about them – 'the joy of the meeting with the newborn Jesus. I desire, dear children, that you live these days as I live them, in joy' (11/12/86).

The season of Lent occasions several reminders from the Blessed Mother about the need to pray, 'from the heart', 'with an active approach', 'before the cross', 'so that you may be witnesses of my presence'. At the same time, we are promised results from our prayer: 'The ice-cold hearts of your brothers and sisters will melt' (23/1/86), 'in order that God's plans for you, and all that God wants through you, may be realized' (30/1/86), 'prayer will be a joy' (20/3/86). We are also asked to live Lent with little sacrifices, and to take Lent as an incentive to change. Mary directly confronts our modern lifestyle: 'Start from this moment. Turn off the television and renounce other things which are useless' (13/2/86).

Conversion This is a major theme. Mary says, 'I rejoice for every child who comes back to me' (14/11/85). Each of us is

called individually to conversion (13/2/86), and we must pray
for the conversion of our neighbours (23/1/86). We are asked
to 'live the messages I give you with humility' (19/9/85,
27/2/86, 17/7/86) and 'witness with your lives' (19/9/85).
This thread of the messages concerning transforming words
into actions is carried further: 'You are speaking but not
acting' (15/5/86). We are to pray, to abandon ourselves to
Mary, to live love, to 'live Holy Mass consciously. Let every
coming to Holy Mass be joyful' (3/4/86); not to be preoccupied with material things, but to witness to Jesus by our lives,
and 'start changing yourselves through prayer and you will
know what to do' (24/4/86).

Love The messages continually speak of love. We are called to
love God, the Virgin Mary, each other, and we are called
to live love (29/5/86, 10/7/86). At the same time we are
assured of Mary's love for us. It is a 'burning love' (29/5/86).
We can overcome sin and every difficulty with love (10/7/86).
Linked to the notion of love is that of light. We are asked to
be 'a light to all' and to 'live the light with your life' (5/6/86).
We are to decide for love, but divine, not human love, and we
are not to be lukewarm and indecisive but must be completely
abandoned to God (20/11/86).

Holiness The Virgin Mary speaks of holiness as a call for
everyone. Her words do not read as a challenge, but as an
encouragement. She appreciates all the prayers and sacrifices
offered. The people will find their way to holiness through
God's grace, and through living the messages, which are 'the
seed of holiness' (10/10/85). Mary stresses how important
family life is for holiness: 'Let your family be a place where
holiness is born' (24/7/86). We are called to holiness, and
have a responsibility to help others to become holy. On 9
October 1986, Mary tells us: 'I desire to lead you on the way
to holiness', and the following month she says that she prays
that we 'begin to live in a holy way, with prayers and sacrifices' (13/11/86). The November messages speak much of
heaven, of Mary's desire that we reach holiness and come to

be with her in heaven: 'Decide today anew for God' (27/11/86) as the way to allowing her to help us.

Peace A major new point is the reference to Medjugorje as an 'oasis of peace' (29/6/86). This may clarify in some ways the plan that Mary is following. From this oasis there can be an effect on the desert, and those in the desert, that is to say the spiritual deserts of the world, will turn towards the oasis. Three of the messages refer to Satan wanting to destroy, to take things to himself, lurking in the desert and wanting to tempt everyone and bring confusion. 'Only by prayer are you able to overcome every influence of Satan' (7/8/86). Our own peace is to help us bring others to peace (25/9/86). We are to pray for peace, and we will obtain peace in praying (23/10/86).

Mary's love for us Mary tells us frequently of her motherly love. 'You know, dear children, I love you immeasurably' (21/8/86). This was the message that made Marija cry because she did not know how to express the idea 'immeasurably' in the sense in which she heard it from the Blessed Virgin. It is important to recognize her love, and the link to her motherhood, both of Jesus, and of ourselves by Jesus' gift. We only have to surrender to it, and Mary is there to help us. 'I am a mediator between you and God' (17/7/86). Thus, we are told, Mary needs our prayers. She cannot help the world without us (28/8/86). Much depends upon us, for she says: 'I am with you but I cannot take away your free will' (7/8/86). We are to bring unity, peace and love to others: 'With love turn everything to good' (31/7/86).

Satan Satan was rarely mentioned in the early messages, but later his name recurs very often: for example, in several of the messages of summer 1985 in connection with his attacks upon the Church, the parish of Medjugorje, the pilgrims, and on individuals. Protection against Satan is assured through the rosary, other prayers and the keeping of blessed objects. There are many significant features here within a few weeks.

Four of the messages mention Satan, and another is about temptation, so that there can be no doubt that Mary is giving the most solemn warning about evil. We are so weak that we need always to be on our guard: 'Take up your arms against Satan, and defeat him with rosaries in your hands' (8/8/85); 'continue praying all the more so that Satan will be driven from this place' (5/9/85). God allows us to be tempted, but he also tests us to allow us the possibility to 'overcome each of these tests calmly' (22/8/85). The cross is the answer to the devil, to temptation, and to every trial. We are unable of our own accord to resist. We need the power of the cross 'from which many graces are coming' (12/9/85).

Purification As the weekly messages near their end, Mary speaks of the Lord's desire 'to cleanse all the sins of your past'. We are to pray to know the evil in us and offer it to the Lord so that he may purify our hearts. 'Pray without ceasing, and prepare your hearts by penance and fasting' (4/12/86). The message of 18 December is one of the most beautiful and consoling, and can only be quoted in full:

> Dear children, again today I want to invite you to prayer. When you pray you are so much more beautiful: like flowers which, after the snow, show all their beauty, and all their colours become indescribable. So also you, dear children, after prayer show in God's sight all the beauty which makes you more dear to him. For this reason, dear children, pray and offer your innermost heart to the Lord, because he makes of you a harmonious and beautiful heavenly flower. Thank you for your response to my call.

In a previous Christmas message Mary had said that each one should bring a flower to the crib. Now it is the people themselves who are to become flowers. There is a progression from symbol to actuality, and it is through prayer that this happens. The last five messages re-emphasize prayer: 'Abandon yourselves totally to me' (11/12/86), 'offer your innermost heart to the Lord' (18/12/86). The final weekly message to the parish is a summary of Mary's requests. It speaks of

41

sacrifices and prayers, of listening to and living the messages, and of Mary's continuing presence with us.

At the end of 1986, Mary was speaking as if she had completed her essential message to the parish. She had done what she was asked to do by God: 'The time has come in which all is complete that my Lord desired' (8/1/87). From this time, she announced, she will give messages at monthly rather than weekly intervals. This is clearly an important milestone in the Medjugorje apparitions, even though the messages will not cease. The teaching of the weekly messages must be seen as having a unity and completeness. In fact Fr George Tutto has pointed out that these messages lasted for 150 weeks, and that they can be meditated upon in sets of ten, like the decades of the rosary. He has undertaken a systematic exploration of the entire set of weekly messages and their scriptural and spiritual dimensions in a series of articles in *MIR* (Peace), the magazine of the Manchester Medjugorje Centre.

The third phase
The monthly messages which began in January 1987 have continued over a longer period than either of the first two phases of the apparitions. It would appear that Mary's purpose has been to develop and reinforce the earlier messages, and to urge everyone who is open to them to live them more fully. Only this can explain the frequent repetitions and variations on the main themes of prayer, making a conscious decision for God, surrender to God, and seeking holiness, protection against Satan, and peace. In April 1987 Mary tells us that God will reveal his plan to us through prayer, and she says: 'Let prayer become your life ... Day in, day out, come as close as you can to God through prayer' (September 1987). All the messages of 1987 speak of prayer either directly or indirectly: we are to pray for others, for graces we need, to be with Jesus, to have protection, to reach perfect love, and to understand Mary's love and God's designs. The Christmas Day message makes a very direct appeal:

I am calling you to sincere prayer of the heart so that your every prayer may be a meeting place with God. Every single day let him take first place in your work and in your life.

During the early months of 1988 all the messages take up the theme of abandonment to God. Never before in her Medjugorje messages had the Blessed Virgin given such prolonged emphasis to a single theme. What can we understand to be the significance of this? Mary says: 'Place your life in God's hands' (January); 'sacrifice your life for the salvation of the world' (February); 'pray in such a way that your prayer and your surrender to God become a signpost' (March); 'let your life be a testimony to the way of holiness' (April); 'I desire that through you the whole world will come to know the God of joy . . . do not be anxious or worried' (May); 'surrender yourselves to God, so that he may heal you, console you and forgive everything inside you which is a hindrance to the way of love' (June). The other aspects of the messages are in close relation to this central theme. We are to have a firm faith (January and April) and will (January); we are being helped to find the road to peace (February and March); we are to pray for our own and others' protection from Satan (February and May); Holy Mass is to be our life (April); we are to accept things which are bitter and difficult, 'for the sake of Jesus, who is love itself' (June).

The messages of the second half of 1988 speak of the many consequences of allowing God 'to take control of your life as the king of all you possess' (July). We will know peace (July). We are to pray for joy and give thanks (August). All are invited to holiness and to bear witness to God (September). We are to give our hearts to Jesus, and consecrate them to his mother 'as persons, as families and as parishes, so that all belong to God through my hands' (October). We are reminded to live the messages so as to be drawn closer to the heart of Jesus, and Mary assures us of her protection:

I do not want anything for myself, but all for the salvation of souls. Satan is strong and therefore you, my little children, by constant prayer press tightly against my motherly heart.' (October)

What is to be the outcome of all the prayer that Mary asks of us? Why does she return again and again to this request? For one thing, it must be that we are not praying enough, and she is behaving like a good mother in reminding us to do what we are supposed to do. But it is surely much more than inculcating a good habit. In her November message she emphasizes the nature of prayer as a joyful encounter with God. There should be a time in each day when we consciously place ourselves fully in his presence. There is thus an element of our choice, of our freedom, as Mary says, that comes into this prayer (November). This gives us nothing to boast of, but rather demonstrates the love and the respect that God has for us, that he wants us to come freely to him. Finally, in December, Mary returns to the theme of peace, the peace that comes from God. 'It is in that peace that I have come as your mother and Queen of Peace.' She is the woman through whom peace has been restored to the world with the birth of Jesus. Her Christmas Day message concludes: 'Today I give you my special blessing. Take it to the whole of creation so that it may know peace.'

The decade of the 1980s concludes with Mary continuing to repeat her advice and to further strengthen her appeals. Though calling us to holiness and to 'be open to everything God is doing through you' (January 1989), she warns us: 'For years now you have been invited to holiness but you are still far away' (March). The tenor of the messages is, however, profoundly hopeful. We are to give thanks and welcome the joy that God gives us. All he asks of us is surrender. Very unusually, the March and April messages start with exactly the same sentence: 'I am calling you to a complete surrender to God.' And then in May she re-emphasizes: 'I invite you to live with God and to surrender completely to him . . . Decide seriously for God because everything else passes away.' In the remaining months of the year, Mary repeats over again the messages of prayer, surrender, joy and peace.

Her wish, she tells us in November, has been 'to make a very beautiful mosaic in your hearts so that I might be able to present each one of you to God, like an original image.'

This work of purification is then re-affirmed in the message of Christmas Day 1989 which takes us into the decade of the 1990s, a time that seems bright with hope on account of all the changes that God's mercy is bringing about in Eastern Europe, but which is also a time of great spiritual need in the world. This message is quoted in full, since it can serve as a summary of the whole sequence of monthly messages of the third phase of the apparitions.

> Dear children, today I am blessing you in a special way with my motherly blessing. I am interceding for you before God that he gives you the gift of conversion of the heart. For years I have been calling you and exhorting you to a deep spiritual life in simplicity, but you are so cold. Therefore, little children, I ask you to accept and live the messages seriously, so that your soul will not be sad when I shall be no longer with you, and when I shall no longer lead you like a child insecure in his first steps. Therefore, little children, read every day the messages that I am giving you, and transform them into your life. I love you, and therefore I am calling you all to the way of salvation with God. Thank you for your response to my call.

Referring to the time when the apparitions will have ended, and when we shall no longer be receiving her messages, Mary assures us of her continuing love and prayers for us. She calls on us to recognize that we have not sufficiently responded. We are cold, and our hearts are not yet converted. Now is the time when we must hear and respond fully to her messages. They are the way that she is calling us to 'salvation with God'.

Mary's call to complete conversion

The principal areas of spiritual development that Mary wants for us and encourages us to seek have been summarized as: prayer, penance, conversion, faith and peace.

Prayer, in its many forms, is the first essential. It includes especially the Mass, the rosary, and family or group prayer, all of which have a transforming power if they become what Mary calls 'prayer of the heart'.

Penance, especially fasting, is a practice that Mary is seeking to restore as a valued part of Christian life to repent for sin and as a way of opening to God.

Conversion is a grace needed continuously by all, including believers, and involves turning to God and seeking his will before our own.

Faith, independently of the apparitions which are just a means by which Mary is bringing those who believe in the Christian faith closer to her son.

Peace as a need of our world that everybody recognizes, but which eludes our efforts, whether in our own hearts, in our families, communities or across the globe, but which can be won by prayer, fasting, conversion of heart and trusting faith. It is the sign that God's kingdom is coming.

The messages are a mine of beautiful counsels and reassurances. They lead to hope, not fear. They show us the way to love and to holiness. Above all they speak to us of our relationship with God which has to be nurtured through our prayer and faithfulness. These urgings reflect many of the prophetic utterances of the Old Testament, of Moses, the psalms, and the prophets. But, more than this, they situate the message of the gospel in the present day. It is possible to be holy in the twentieth century, but not of our own strength. We have to hand all our weaknesses to God, and seek to serve him through our sacrifices, our love of family and neighbour, and our participation in the life of the Church. Whatever our weaknesses, we can remain hopeful because he loves us, and we can be encouraged by the knowledge that Mary is there to help and guide us. Beyond that, there is a world to save, a world loved by God, but which has forsaken him. It must be the concern of God's people to pray and help others to come to know God, but this can only occur through the power of the cross and the inspiration of the Holy Spirit.

Now we face a situation in which Mary is calling on the whole of humanity to turn back to God. She is being allowed to repeat on a world scale the message given originally by her son to a few thousand people in Israel. She speaks as a mother, not as a scientist or a theologian, and yet what she says directly challenges worldly wisdom. We know that we live in a world that lacks any shared view of meaning and purpose. We can see that the banishing of God from everyday life is virtually complete, at least in the West, and that this leaves us prey to love of self; there is nothing else but self. It is this idolatry that Mary has come to warn against. She is asking us to turn our whole world around, and to seek first the kingdom of God. This is a radical challenge. Our world sets its heart on other goals. By all the evidence God is the last thing on very many minds.

Is this miracle of conversion likely? No. Is it possible? Humanly speaking, no. The only hope lies with God himself. That is, only prayer and not human efforts will bring about the miracle of conversion, but it will occur only as far as we respond to the messages of Medjugorje or to the gospel which underlies them. The messages that we are being asked to live run parallel to the psalms, the gospel, and the great prophecies of the Old Testament. As a prophet, Mary is unparalleled, for she is the Mother of God, but in so many ways does she come in the line of the prophets that the Church has called her their Queen.

5

The Impact of the Apparitions

The village of Medjugorje

Those who have known Medjugorje since the early years of the apparitions have seen many changes take place. Some of these are simply the result of a small village becoming a tourist centre with hundreds of thousands of visitors each year. The building of hotels or extensions to local homes to provide rooms for rent, and the mushrooming of cafés and souvenir shops are what might be expected anywhere as increasing numbers of people arrive. My first visit to Medjugorje at the beginning of 1984 preceded all such developments. There was nowhere to buy food, and nowhere to stay because at that time foreigners were not being allowed to stay in villagers' homes. I found accommodation in the nearest town and walked or hitched to Medjugorje each day. Even today, however, the religious sites have scarcely changed. A new approach road to the village is gradually being completed, but the church has not changed other than by having a piazza laid out in front and an impressive public address system installed. The presbytery is unchanged. The roads leading off to Podbrdo, the hill of the apparitions, and Krizevac, the hill of the cross, are the same, even if they are lined by many new buildings. The paths up the two hills have been worn by many more feet, and new stations of the cross have been erected on Krizevac, the cross-topped hill that towers over the village, but the climb in the heat of the day or in the depths of night is the same spiritually uplifting experience.

What has changed has been the people, both the villagers and the visitors. The former parish priest, Fr Tomislav Pervan, once said in an interview that it was 'a case of before the apparitions and since the apparitions'. Before, far fewer went to church and many families in the various hamlets of the village were divided by disputes over land ownership and other quarrels. The young people hardly knew traditional prayers, and many showed little conviction about the faith which had been so strong in their native Croatia over the centuries. The priests of the parish had become dispirited, as Father Vlasic has frequently recounted when speaking of the beginning of the apparitions.

But once the apparitions started, and people began to believe in them, the life of the village was completely transformed. In 1984, it was apparent to the visitor that the local people were very devout. The church was full every night of the week during the time I was there, even though the January weather was very cold and wet. Fr Jozo Zovko, the parish priest at the time of the first apparitions, has described how families of the village became reconciled to each other, how they gave up bad language, how the men returned to church, and how the people began to pray in their homes, in the fields, on Podbrdo and on Krizevac. Then pilgrims started to come, and the villagers had to make room for them in the church, and later in their homes. In 1986 I found that many householders did not even charge visitors for staying, or they accepted whatever pilgrims offered, but the authorities imposed a specially severe tourist tax which forced compliance with a more commercial approach.

But the transformation went well beyond this. There was a fundamental spiritual revival in the village. People were really praying, really believing. Visitors sensed this, and were edified by the contact with the villagers. Many pilgrims during the early days have reported how the one thing that struck them from their visit to Medjugorje was the attitude of the local people. It had quickly come to be accepted by most of them that Mary was guiding them to develop a fuller parish and community life, indeed a model parish life to be a witness to the wider world. Through the Thursday messages over the period 1984–87 the villagers were aware that they had a task to perform. They were to pray much more, to fast, to be reconciled to one another, and to be patient and tolerant despite all problems, such as the difficulties the parish had with the local bishop who disputed the authenticity of the apparitions, and with the increasing numbers of pilgrims who were bringing major changes to the life of the village.

Pilgrims returning to Medjugorje confirm that this spiritual atmosphere has remained and has even developed over the years despite the huge increase in the numbers of people present. Can there be a parish in the whole world where the liturgy is celebrated with such faith and devotion as in Medjugorje? It is a place where prayer is literally unceasing. No matter what time of the day or night, there is either a Mass in progress, the rosary being said, or people are praying before the Blessed Sacrament, making the stations of the cross, praying in groups on the hills or in their homes. A background buzz of prayer can often be heard as the visitor walks down a lane between a group of houses. It is a place where, as one pilgrim said to me, 'the Spirit is moving'.

Medjugorje is a Franciscan parish. The priests who have been called to serve there have constituted a very talented group, despite the personnel changes that have frequently occurred as a result of misgivings by church and civil authorities. A tiny village in the middle of Croatia, not to be found on the map being issued to travellers by the Yugoslav Tourist Office in 1984, has been able to count among its priests several theologians, a psychotherapist, an exorcist and several superlative linguists, as well as inspiring preachers and spiritual directors. Only with such resources could the parish have coped with the inflow of pilgrims, who were coming from every level of society and culture, many of them with great spiritual needs. Visiting priests, either local Franciscans or pilgrims from elsewhere, were increasingly called upon to assist in the work, to the point that, less than five years after the apparitions began, it had become nothing unusual to see as many as fifty priests hearing confessions simultaneously on the 'lawn of mercy' beside the church, or as many as 200 priests concelebrating Mass on a feast-day evening.

The major enduring human feature of Medjugorje, however, has been the personalities and spiritual strength of the visionaries themselves. Hardly anyone fails to be impressed by the faith, joy and peace evident in the visionaries in the way they cope with the onslaught of crowds of people wanting to talk to them, to be prayed with, or to ask questions and favours. This routine is continuous from early morning until night-time, and yet Marija and Vicka, who have borne the brunt of it, never show impatience or fail to have a word of consolation for pilgrims. Ivan is known for a sense of humour that can verge on the caustic when he is provoked, as in the case of the pilgrim who asked: 'Can you tell us something about the secrets?' I heard him answer swiftly, with a smile: 'If I did, they wouldn't be secrets.'

It is known that all the visionaries have a personal prayer life that responds fully to the request that Mary is making of them, that is at least three hours of prayer daily; and they are known to fast on bread and water, two, and at times more, days a week. The most illuminating opportunity for most pilgrims to observe the visionaries' qualities for themselves is when gathering in front of their houses to hear them pray and speak spontaneously with whoever comes. Any kind of question can come up, and yet they always seem to have a response with substance to it, or they put the question back to the questioner with something new to reflect on. I heard Marija asked by a pilgrim: 'How should we pray?' She answered:

The form is not important, as long as you pray with the heart. At the beginning I did not always feel like praying, but you make up your own prayers and you warm up, like a child learning to walk.

The fact that relatively uneducated teenagers, which is what they were when the apparitions began, have been able to keep up this exchange for years with adult pilgrims, often including experienced pastors and theologians, is surely one of the clearest signs of the authenticity of the apparitions.

In the development of the parish of Medjugorje, one of the main strands has been the reconciliation of young people to the faith. Prayer groups began to form among the young, as a direct response to a request of the Blessed Virgin. One of these groups, associated with Jelena, has had a significant influence upon the spiritual renewal being stimulated by Medjugorje. Under the pastoral care of Father Vlasic, but with the young Jelena guiding it through the inner locutions she receives from the Virgin, this group has been in existence since 1983. Its meetings have been private, lengthy and frequent, that is, usually for two to three hours, twice a week. The core of the group has remained constant over this time, and a subgroup spent five months on retreat in Italy in 1987, during the Marian Year. Now the group is evolving into a new form of religious community, still under the guidance of Father Vlasic (Vlasic, 1988). At the moment one could only speculate what might be the wider impact of this development, since it had hitherto been assumed by many that the young people of the prayer group would disperse into conventional religious orders and seminaries if they chose to follow a religious life.

Spiritual renewal

Broadly it can be said that the impact of the apparitions and messages has been to provide the inspiration for a spiritual renewal, as was mentioned in chapter four, to provide a spiritual rule of life for the parish and for whoever else wishes to follow it. Although it is not formally detailed, other than in the various messages of the Blessed Virgin that bear upon aspects of the spiritual life, and also in the published sermons and meditations of Father Vlasic and Father Barbaric with their profound reflections on the messages, it may be helpful to set out this rule as it can be seen to be lived by Medjugorje parishioners and pilgrims:

The Mass is central, with daily attendance being normal. There is also strong emphasis upon adoration of the Blessed Sacrament exposed on the altar, especially on Thursdays;

the characteristic Medjugorje prayers since the beginning have been the seven 'Our Father's, 'Hail Mary's and 'Glory be's for peace, and the Creed;

the complete rosary, joyful, sorrowful and glorious mysteries, daily, and as a family prayer where possible;

morning and evening prayer, in the family where possible;

a total prayer time extending to about three hours a day;

reading from the Bible daily, and the passage from Matthew (6:24–34) on Thursdays;

fasting on bread and water on Wednesdays and Fridays.

When she was asked about the demanding nature of some of these practices, the Virgin Mary said that these were not too much, since they still only required a small portion of each day, and that if we knew how much we were loved by God we would be praying all the time. It is a common experience in Medjugorje to find a new capacity for prayer. The village has been called a 'school of prayer' (Tutto, 1986), and it would seem that we should see this spiritual rule not as a set of rules to be obeyed mechanically, but as a guide towards a life closer to God.

If prayer and fasting have followed this guide, then the living of the messages for which Mary so often asks can more easily develop. Here an additional word may be needed. Even for some who accept and follow the messages about prayer, those about fasting can still cause some difficulty. Yet fasting is not spoken of by Mary as an ascetic practice, as a kind of self-punishment or a painful experience. It is seen rather as the opening of a door to God's presence. It is a way of simplifying life, a form of detachment and poverty of spirit, which opens up the possibility of greater solidarity with the poor and increases the intercessory value of prayer. The power of fasting stems from its association with the cross and from fellowship with Jesus' suffering.

Continuous conversion

But prayer and fasting are only the beginning of what the Mother of God is asking. She calls us to conversion, which means that we should not pray and fast merely to conform to a rule, but because of our commitment to God. Mary constantly urges us to a deliberate and conscious decision for God, a continuous conversion. Through prayer, fasting and conversion, many have found the grace really to know God in faith, to have a profound conviction about the Eucharist, to accept Mary as their mother, and to be able to rely upon divine protection from evil. This renewed spiritual life brings peace to the hearts of individuals, their families and their communities, and it culminates in salvation, where God will be experienced to the full potential of our spiritual nature.

Pilgrims and witnesses

In the past several years I have heard or read a large number of accounts of pilgrimages to Medjugorje, but it is always personal experience that counts the most. I first went to Medjugorje in thanksgiving for my return to faith after a lapse of fifteen years. I read a newspaper article about the apparitions in 1983, and immediately felt a lively interest. Six weeks later I went on pilgrimage alone, sure that I would find some spiritual truth. I remember vividly the excitement of approaching Medjugorje, the disconcerting emptiness of the village when I arrived, the way the church filled to capacity in the evening, the cold, bright January sun at noontime on the hill of the apparitions, and the hours spent in reflection and prayer which seemed so inviting and fruitful. I had no extraordinary sensory experience, such as many other pilgrims have recounted, but I can affirm that I was given a spiritual awakening and impulsion that are still with me despite all the vagaries of my character and life. It is the innumerable accounts from Medjugorje pilgrims that tell a similar story that must in the end, I believe, ensure the Church's approval for the apparitions.

The fact is that had anybody told me a year earlier that I would be making a pilgrimage to a place of Marian apparitions, or that I would be absorbed in three hours of church services for several nights in succession, and that I would be publishing an article about it in *The Guardian* within the year, I would have thought only that they were totally deluded. My search at the time was through the *est* training, a Californian awareness programme which had no specifically religious content even though it had a flavour of eastern spirituality about it. Perhaps this spiritual dimension served to awaken my dormant curiosity about religion, but in any case it was my original Catholicism that reasserted itself, suddenly and firmly. What my first visit to Medjugorje brought me, as I now see it, was a new awareness of God and a sense of conviction and commitment as to the primacy of the spiritual dimension in life.

Many have reported their spiritual response to the experience of Medjugorje, while others have been inspired purely by hearing about the apparitions of the Virgin Mary and beginning to live the messages without even making a pilgrimage. Some have even undergone sudden conversions simply on hearing of the events. For example, a letter sent to the Medjugorje Centre in London in 1988 read, in part:

> I wrote to the Centre soon after the 'Everyman' programme last February and obtained a book on the happenings at Medjugorje. I flicked through it and stopped at a picture of the twin-towered church there. I then started crying, the tears literally dropping onto the page. I have told many people of my experience, to try and get them interested in Our Lady's message. Apart from blank stares and incredulous looks, I quote two verbal reactions: 'They (probably meaning the Catholic Church) must have sensitized the page in the book', and the other: 'The human brain is a strange and complex thing.' (*Medjugorje Messenger*, no. 10)

A similar experience was that of Igor, a young Italian who described himself as 'in the grip of drugs, sensuality and many

other things the world offers so freely to young people'. Help
first came to him through his mother.

> My mother brought home a book, *Our Lady of Medjugorje*,
> and suggested I read it. I opened it, read the introduction,
> and flicked through the pages, but was stopped by these
> words: 'I am your mother and what I want for you is
> peace, peace, peace.' I needed that peace at that moment. I
> became upset and wanted to cry . . . and I did cry . . . and
> the truth entered my heart at that moment. (*Mirecorder*, no.
> 13)

Nor can it be denied that large numbers of conversions have
occurred among pilgrims drawn to Medjugorje by their state
of spiritual need, or by their desire to discover for themselves
whether the apparitions were genuine.

> Two of our group, a husband and wife, were from Belfast.
> They were a lovely couple and about three months pre-
> viously their fifteen-year-old daughter had been tragically
> killed in a motor accident. On the first day the woman was
> very emotional. After a powerful spiritual experience the
> woman was a changed person for the rest of the trip. That
> night was the first occasion that she had really slept well
> and she did not call for her daughter any more. (*Medjugorje
> Messenger*, no. 2)

And a young man's personal account:

> Before going to Medjugorje I had wondered what on earth
> I was going to do for four whole days . . . My only reason
> for going was one of idle curiosity . . . I proceeded to spend
> the next four days in what I can only describe as the most
> magical place I could ever have dreamt of going to. Anyone
> who has read the C. S. Lewis books that centre around the
> mythical land of Narnia will know what I mean when I
> talk about a place that has Real Stillness, Real Beauty,
> Real Serenity and where the presence of God is so strong
> that it pervades every moment of your precious time there.
> It is a place that has Christ as its centre, at its core. The

beauty of Medjugorje lies not only in its mountains and its landscape, but in the very real sense of timelessness that you feel when you are there. Life there has a simplicity which is crucial to this feeling of timelessness revolving around work, prayer, eating together, sleep and going to Mass. The effect of this experience was to give me a belief in God that I never thought I would have. It made me realize how shallow my belief had been before, and it showed me how through prayer I could bring myself close to God if I so wished. (*Medjugorje Messenger*, no. 7)

An unwilling seeker, Ben, who had gone to Medjugorje mainly to accompany his girlfriend, discovered his own reason for being there. He stated his conviction that 'the biggest miracles are the miracles that happen in people to take them a step closer to Jesus. I hope I've taken one or two steps in Medjugorje, and the miracle belongs to God.' He described his experience:

Conversion is never easy. When our Blessed Mother calls us to conversion she calls us to devotion, devotion to her son. Being a Christian involves devotion, devotion in prayer and in accepting and trying to live up to the life of Christ. This was something I did not realize before my recent trip to Medjugorje. My relationship to God was that of trying to satisfy my intellectual curiosity. Trying to rationalize and understand the truth of God, rather than accepting and loving him. Not being in the Catholic Church, I tended to look at the superficial aspects and to be highly critical of all the ceremonial and objects involved in worship . . . So when the seeker comes to the end of his intellectual tether and is in need of conversion (devotion to Christ and acceptance of all he has to offer) he suffers much conflict and doubt, so much conflict and doubt that God seems lost to him. (*Medjugorje Messenger*, no. 4)

Ben was later received into the Catholic Church and has entered the Franciscan order. Some of the conversions reported, from Judaism, from agnosticism or from atheism, are really nothing short of road-to-Damascus experiences. Shortly after her return from Medjugorje in March 1987 I met June who, before her visit, was not a Catholic, knew only one other person in her group, was travelling simply to have a holiday trip with her friend, and had never heard of Medjugorje. She explains, in her written account:

> Somewhere along the line, in spite of a loving husband, three children and many material benefits, I had lost myself and all sense of direction . . . Once in Medjugorje, I watched the people who walked by and the expression on their faces confirmed my worst fears. They were probably 'high' and I was in the midst of some hippie community. I also had an uncomfortable feeling that 'they', the rest of the party, were after my soul, which I would resist at all costs.

When June and her friend climbed up the hill of the cross, they stopped at the first station.

> Suddenly, I felt as if something was urging me to look up at the sun. I looked up and, instead of blinding me, the heat from the sun flowed backwards, and the sun was just a silver ball in the sky. The sun then became eclipsed by a midnight, almost navy-blue disc, with a silver edging of sparkling light. Then it began to beat, backwards and forwards in the sky. A massive heart pounding powerfully, with a whirligig of the most beautiful colours swirling around it. Shades of blue, green, yellow, orange and pink. A cloud of pink detached itself from the colours around the sun and drifted, like smoke from a chimney, across the sky and wrapped itself around the cross of the second station. Other colours appeared on the rocks and the thorn bushes – blues and greens. The whole scene before our eyes (Donna and I were both seeing the same things) was incredibly beautiful. A shaft of light came down towards me, the shaft silver and the edges tinged with blue.
> Not only was I seeing with my eyes, but I was being touched to the very depths of my soul. Love and peace were coming towards me and entering into me and I became part

of the love. A speck standing in eternity, a nothing, yet something because of God and his love for us all. I knew I was seeing and feeling the impossible, but anything and everything was possible with God. Love, peace, beauty, no darkness, no fear, no death, no decay, no shadows. Everything was true. God, Jesus, the Holy Spirit, Mary – my undefined belief turned to knowledge. When I turned and looked behind me, the whole world had changed. There was no darkness, everything looked newly washed, colours glowed, my vision was crystal clear. 'I was blind, but now I see.' (*Medjugorje Messenger*, no. 7)

A few months after her visit to Medjugorje June was received into the Catholic Church, and her husband, a former Catholic, returned to the practice of his faith, and they had their marriage solemnized in church.

Billy, a nominal Christian from Scotland, went to Medjugorje in May 1985, after seeing a video about the apparitions that had a big impact on him. He had not been to church for two years when he attended Mass on his first morning in Medjugorje. Although not a Catholic, he describes his response in his own words:

I became aware of the true presence of Christ at the Mass and especially in the sacramental host, the body of Christ, but I was unable to receive it because I was a Protestant. For as long as I had been praying, I had been asking God over the years to show me the true Church – if there was one on earth at this time. Since I had started to fast and pray over the last few months, I had asked him to use me in whatever way he chose, his will not mine. I had a great desire to pray in Medjugorje, and to attend Mass or go up the mountain. I would climb the mountain every night at midnight and pray for the people back home; it was so peaceful up there at night!

One night we were invited up the Hill of the Apparitions to be with the visionaries. There was a prayer group of about thirty people singing and playing guitars. The singing stopped, we said the rosary, and after this the four visionaries got up and knelt before a wooden cross and started to pray out loud. I looked up at the stars; the full moon was just rising over the hill to my left. I saw what I first thought to be a shooting star, with a small tail behind. This star came level with my eyes and did a ninety-degree turn downwards, only to vanish in front of me. As soon as it vanished, the visionaries stopped praying and started having the vision. Throughout the vision, which lasted about ten minutes, I was aware of an overpowering fragrance of flowers which had not been there before; there were only rocks and gorse bushes around. I have never felt so much at peace as I did at that moment; my whole insides were flowing and tingling and I thought I never wanted to lose this feeling. I was not shocked in the least and accepted it all as Our Lord's glory. I did not know until afterwards that I was the only person who saw this. I felt then, and still do, so privileged to have had this experience. Since that moment, Our Lady has meant much more to me and I ask her to help me pray to her son Jesus Christ in my prayers. My wife and I say the holy rosary or pray every day now.

More was to come. The next day Billy was introduced to Sr Briege McKenna outside the church. He did not know of her prayer and healing ministry (McKenna, 1987). His account continues:

Sister Briege turned to look at me, eye to eye; she instantly took hold of my right hand with her left hand, and her right hand she laid on my heart. As soon as she started to pray, I started to cry, the first time for ten years. My legs started shaking, and my heart started thumping like a hammer. I didn't know what was happening to me. She said: 'Billy, Jesus is telling me that when you go home, you've to start taking instruction to become a Catholic.' And I knew in my heart that she was speaking the truth.

After returning to Medjugorje two months later with his wife, Carole, and a young daughter, Billy and his family began to prepare to be received into the Catholic Church. They are now devoted Catholics, and it was on a further pilgrimage to Medjugorje at Easter 1989 which I shared with them that I heard from them about their experience.

Spiritual and physical healing

Some of the most extraordinary accounts come from people who were ill, physically or emotionally. The video *Dear Children*, which was made in 1987 by Ernest Williams, included the testimonies of several young people who had been released from drug addiction in Medjugorje. The *Mirecorder* published the story of David Hunt, from Zimbabwe, who had been a hard-drugs addict for twelve years.

> All I had found was despair, bitterness, confusion, social alienation and isolation and the most ugly and overwhelming sense of guilt and self-hatred that left no room for God, happiness or peace . . . I have no hesitation in stating that I received a very definite spiritual and physical healing in Medjugorje, and while this healing may have been outwardly invisible, the serenity and comfort it encouraged, the renewal of faith it inspired deep within me, was (and I pray always will be) something undeniably explosive . . . and for this I thank God and the Queen of Peace . . . I am convinced that the true spiritual message of Medjugorje is one of great joy, hope, comfort and encouragement to all mankind – particularly those whose lives are entangled in the worldly web of materialism, confusion, pain, despair, guilt, loneliness, sorrow, etc., and who are searching for a faith and a God to strengthen and uplift their spirit, and to bring peace of mind. (*Mirecorder*, no. 10)

Miracles of healing like those at Lourdes are not lacking. Many such cases have been reported, including that of Agnes Heupel, who was cured after twelve years of paralysis at Medjugorje on the vigil of the Feast of Our Lady of Fatima, 12 May 1986. Another case, whose medical record is before me as I write, is that of Rita Klaus, of Evans City, Pennsylvania, who had had multiple sclerosis for twenty-six years, with complete paralysis of both feet and ankles and structural deformities of both legs. She had read René Laurentin's book *Is the Virgin Mary Appearing at Medjugorje?* (Laurentin, 1984), and began fasting several days a week. One evening at home in the United States she had been praying the rosary when she had the idea of asking Jesus for a cure through the intercession of the Virgin of Medjugorje. She writes:

> I had never prayed for a cure before – only that I would always do God's will, do it well and do it happily. As I asked Mary, our Mother, to intercede for me, I felt a sudden surge of 'electricity' through me . . . I went to sleep immediately.

It was the next morning, after attending a class, that she noticed that her legs were straight.

> I was so overjoyed I cried out, yelled my thanks to God and Mary. I took off my braces and using the crutches went to the bottom of the flight of stairs which leads to the second floor. I said to myself, 'If I am cured, I can run up those stairs.' I ran up the stairs! Then I ran all over the place!

Rita's physician, Dr Angel Viera, had been seeing her at ninety-day intervals. His most recent report, dated 17 April, has the entry: 'Final diagnoses: quadriparesis secondary to multiple sclerosis involving mainly lower extremities; neurogenic bowel and bladder, obesity.' After the consultation he gave her on 23 June, he writes: 'The patient is presently ambulating totally independent of any equipment and has regained full strength of both lower extremities . . . She could hop on one leg or the other with her eyes open . . . I am not sure where to place her recovery in such a short period of time but I think I would not question her recovery.'

According to Rita, he had said: 'Go home, go to church, and thank God.' Subsequently to this, Rita's three brothers and her sister returned to the practice of their Catholic faith, and all their children were under instruction to receive baptism. She concludes her account:

> Never has our family experienced such joy and peace. There is no way I can ever express my gratitude to heaven for all the blessings we have received through our Mother's intercession.

The apparitions and the Church

The events of Medjugorje are intensively church-centred. The authority of the parish clergy over the daily life of the parish is spiritually very secure. The daily life of the parish revolves not around the visionaries and their apparitions, but the Mass. One of the striking features of Medjugorje for pilgrims is the beauty and intense holiness of the Mass, and especially the evening liturgy which follows a series of foreign-language Masses for pilgrims during the day. This is the time when the church is most crowded, but when there is also the greatest conviction of worship. The Eucharist is central to the parish life of Medjugorje. Whether in the Mass or in the eucharistic worship at times of exposition and benediction, the affirmation of belief in the real presence of Jesus on the altar is tangible. Many pilgrims have commented on this. For example, one wrote in a letter to the London Medjugorje Centre:

> One unforgettable impression was the Mass on 26 June 1985. I saw true worship there that night, true reverence and true love for the Mass. At the consecration the priest held up the host, a great white host, looking like the moon. He held it up to the people, and all in unison they whispered 'Jesus', and a shiver ran through me because I had never felt the real presence of Jesus in the Mass before. (*Medjugorje Messenger*, no. 1)

The effect of Mary's teaching has been to reinforce this attitude of centring the spiritual life on the Mass, eucharistic adoration and private prayer before the Blessed Sacrament.

Developments in Medjugorje have been occurring so rapidly that church authorities have been taken completely by surprise and have been uncertain how to respond. In the meantime, estimates of the number of pilgrims to have visited Medjugorje range as high as twelve millions, though there is no way of accurately assessing this figure. A recent report from the Franciscans in Medjugorje revealed that there were a million communions in 1988, that 12,000 priests had signed the presbytery register, and that sixty bishops visited Medjugorje in 1988 (*Catholic Herald*, May 1989). Pilgrimages are being organized from all parts of the world, and these include non-Catholic groups such as an Anglican charismatic party from England (*Medjugorje Messenger*, no. 8). Returning pilgrims have set up networks to help spread the messages. They have started magazines, have shown videos, organized prayer groups and public meetings, canvassed the clergy, written newspaper articles and books, prayed and fasted.

The strong faith which is characteristic of Medjugorje pilgrims is having its effects throughout the Church. The spiritual discipline for which Mary is asking is challenging the whole movement of disintegration of Christianity into rationalist or science-based views of the world. The power of prayer with fasting is being re-emphasized. Priests from Medjugorje visiting other countries can draw thousands to public meetings to speak about the rosary, fasting, and prayer of the heart. I have, for example, the personal memory of an extraordinary day of prayer led by Fr Slavko Barbaric of Medjugorje at Banneux, Belgium, on 11 December 1988, which was attended by more than 5,000 people, including a bishop and fifty priests. One of the priests present wrote afterwards: 'Before the day at Banneux I would have said "Wait for the judgement of the Church". Today my response is "Go and tell what you have seen and heard" ' (*Nouvelles de Medjugorje*, February 1989).

6

Opposition to Medjugorje and the Messages

Since it is the characteristic of prophetic messages that they go to the heart of the matter, challenging existing ideas and practice, it is not surprising that they almost invariably encounter opposition. Several New Testament sources tell us of the fate that awaits those who proclaim the message of Jesus, that they will be hated, rejected, forbidden the synagogue, or brought before courts of judgement. That this happens cannot of course be claimed as an indication of the truth of the message, but it is almost a counter-indication if there is no opposition. Negative reactions were to be expected in the case of the apparitions and messages at Medjugorje, since these place a spiritual question mark over many contemporary values and ways of living. Such responses should therefore be examined to see whether they negate the validity of the claimed spiritual phenomena, or whether indeed they tend to confirm their truth. That is, is the opposition truly a discouragement to faith in the messages or does it lead us to recognize in Medjugorje a genuine movement of the Holy Spirit? These are, of course, matters of interpretation, but I believe that this chapter, which seeks to confront such opposition without polemic, is an important element of the book, because it suggests the hopeful conclusion that disapproval for the Medjugorje phenomena and associated spiritual messages is largely ill-conceived or suspect.

The authenticity of Medjugorje has been questioned in very principle from the beginning. One form of opposition sees itself as virtuous in Christian terms, as protecting the integrity of the faith and preventing it from being diluted by nonessentials. A manifestation of this is the view that is character-istically anti-Marian, which sees devotion to the Virgin Mary as deviant or heretical. Chapter three represented an attempt to show that the alleged Mariolatry of the Catholic Church does not correspond to reality. Official doctrine does not support it, and the eucharistic devotion in Medjugorje is firmly Christocentric. Of course many modern minds will repudiate even such traditional orthodoxy. Since we live at a time of deference to scientific rationalism rather than to religious faith, disbelief in any supernatural reality or inter-vention in human life is probably greater than it has ever been. It is therefore not surprising that there are even many religious leaders whose purpose is to reinterpret and explain away divine truths. This leads to a second response, which is to discuss such phenomena as Medjugorje as if they were curious social and psychological realities rather than spiritual ones. The media, for example, have proved incapable of deal-ing with Medjugorje on its own terms; at best they can inform, often reluctantly and usually misleadingly, and the net effect is to be dismissive. And a third form of opposition is the most implacable: the opposition that reflects the conflict between good and evil in creation.

Virtuous opposition

There is disagreement, even confusion over the apparitions, within the Catholic Church itself, with many lay people, priests and bishops visiting Medjugorje as pilgrims, while the official Church remains undecided and leaves many with the impression that this hesitation is tantamount to disapproval. It is well known that the Bishop of Mostar, in whose diocese Medjugorje is located, has taken a position against the authenticity of the apparitions. Even the parish of Medjugorje becoming a worldwide centre of pilgrimage has not persuaded him to change his view, and his example has been followed by other bishops who have spoken against Medjugorje or attempted to restrain, or even oppose, the propagation of the Medjugorje messages.

The normal way for such matters to be dealt with is for the local bishop to make inquiry in order to guide the wider Church. In this case, however, the initial inquiry by a diocesan commission was not acceptable to the Vatican authorities, and the result has been that the Bishop of Mostar has lost his jurisdiction over the case. The Church's view will now be formed from the deliberations of a national commission of the Yugoslav Bishops' Conference which has yet to submit its conclusions. It must be said that even those who are strongly favourable to Medjugorje have reason to be glad of the Church's traditionally firm line over the authentication of apparitions. No Catholic could in conscience wish for a lax attitude from the Church in such matters. It would do little good for the faith of the people if the Church were to confuse its members by stating at one moment that alleged miraculous happenings were worthy of belief and not contrary to the Church's teaching, and then retracting this judgement the next.

However, what the Church has to go on as evidence, where apparitions are claimed, comes from the beliefs, testimony and spiritual response of the people. There is no other basis upon which a judgement can be based. It is therefore unreasonable to expect that any spiritual response should be inhibited while inquiries are in progress, for that could be to impede the work of God and would in any case remove the very evidence upon which the judgement has eventually to be made. This is the argument regarding Medjugorje that has been put by Canon Laurentin and others who have amassed empirical evidence of many kinds, including medical and scientific testimonies concerning the visionaries, physical healings and the luminous phenomena (Joyeux and Laurentin, 1987).

The other ecclesiastical dimension to the whole question is the opposition to Medjugorje and to Marian devotion in general that can stem from fears that such manifestations are either theologically unsound, ecumenically embarrassing, or unnecessary. Those seeking to spread the messages of Medjugorje have at times encountered indifference and even suspicion among parish clergy and church leaders. Indeed, some priests suggest in good faith that women should not allow themselves to be influenced any longer by those whom they see as using the Virgin Mary as a model to reinforce the 'weak' side of women. The Church, it is argued, needs women to bring their contribution and qualities to bear upon its way of being. This response ignores the fact that there are also priests who are unsympathetic to Marian devotion. While a devotion to the Blessed Virgin that manipulates her to subdue women is unacceptable, because it is fundamentally unChristian, the alternative does not have to be to reject out of hand any cult of Mary.

Moreover, any feminist approach needs to avoid undermining those qualities of the Blessed Virgin that cut across sexual and class categories. We are all called to holiness, that is, to accept God's will, to love and serve him, and to care for others generously. Mary did exactly these things. Can it not therefore be acknowledged that the Church has much to learn from women, and that the example of Mary can benefit both the Church and women? Mary's quality is that she can be appealed to to soften the attitudes of priests resistant to 'feminine' qualities in the Church. Among the things Mary has said in Medjugorje are that priests should be models of faith for the people, that they should pray the rosary to protect the Church, and that they should teach the people to pray. Is Mary not simply the one who wishes most passionately to lead people to Jesus, and might not such an attitude be the way to an authentic Marian devotion – not sentimental but definitely with the qualities of heart associated with the feminine?

These matters were reviewed by Pope Paul VI with a sensitive concern for views held in other Christian traditions in his encyclical letter *Marialis Cultus* (Paul VI, 1974). He announces his desire to avoid any tendency 'to separate devotion to the Blessed Virgin Mary from its necessary point of reference – Christ' (Paul VI, 1974, para. 4), but he declares his sympathy with the liturgical renewal that, 'in harmony with tradition, has recognized the singular place that belongs to (the Virgin Mary) in Christian worship as the holy Mother of God and the worthy Associate of the Redeemer' (Paul VI, 1974, para. 15). Pope Paul sees the Virgin Mary as becoming, 'even if only slowly, not an obstacle but a path and a rallying-point of all who believe in Christ' (Paul VI, 1974, para. 33).

Reasoned opposition

No less a difficulty arises in the recognition of spiritual reality when faith is accorded to rationalist viewpoints which approach all questions as capable of being answered either by reason or not at all. The ways of God are not excepted, and thus the rationalist is enmeshed in seeking to analyse the activities of the one who works in veiled ways, who is more easily understood in paradox than through intellectual efforts to penetrate mysteries or to prove the unprovable. Modern culture persists in exhibiting blindness and ignorance about spiritual realities. Either there is no room for a spiritual dimension, or the spiritual is reduced to an aesthetic, a mode of self-flattery that, if scrutinized, can be completely accounted for in social and psychological terms.

Assumptions that discount the transcendental may have had some persuasiveness at a time when the Churches were in decline and had lost credibility for historical reasons such as their being too tied up with the social and political establishment. This was the atmosphere of the mid-1960s when secular optimism was at its apogee. Present conditions are quite different. There is an increasingly widespread search for values and purposes that can transcend personal interest, and this partly as a consequence of the disillusioning nature of materialism itself. In practice, this search often shows itself as an undisciplined gorging on novelties. A whole new field of humanistic, psychological and mystical inquiry has grown up, but it is fragmented and lacks profound roots because it has not recognized its true source in the Absolute.

Rationalist arguments thus unwittingly promote untruth. What are regarded as liberating propositions or definitive advances in civilization can be profoundly erroneous when they lead to the condemning of the notion of commandments of God as obscurantist, authoritarian or simplistic, without being able to take into account its basic premise of faith. Discouragement, and even ridicule, for those who believe literally in the truths of faith are encountered even among Christians, while the media constantly bring to the fore churchmen who seek to reconcile belief and unbelief by conflating faith and reason. If the resurrection is explained away, why not the incarnation? And then what is left? If we accept an attitude of indifference towards truths of the gospel, why should we be concerned about moral absolutes, or even about principles that might offer us rules of conduct in matters of life and death, such as abortion, human embryo experimentation, homosexual relations, substance addition, suicide, and so forth? In trying to rationalize religious faith we are obliged not only to explain away phenomena like Medjugorje but also all those notions that rely utterly upon the transcendental realities of pure love, prayer, hope, holiness and truth.

Such discussion puts God in quotation marks. He becomes an unknown, one who is not on the same level as all the immediacies and certainties of the world. This attitude results in the setting up of a model of humanity without God, humanism in fact, which is an ideal of which God does not form the essential part. Thus there is either an assumption that personal freedom is the greatest good, or the issue of moral evil is dismissed by rationalization or relativism. But the power to discern evil can only come from God. Without an Absolute, how can people know whether the way they have chosen is *better* than an alternative, or even whether such a question has any meaning? And, consequently, what *reason* do they have to be hopeful, or to expect that anyone else should agree with their choice?

Powers of evil

It has also been apparent that there is opposition to Medjugorje that is of another order. The frequent references in Mary's messages to the power of Satan in the world, the incidence of exorcisms in Medjugorje itself, and the struggles of those involved in the spiritual work stemming from Medjugorje to maintain peace and harmony in the face of misleading reports in the media, clashes of personality and interpretation, and even disagreements among devotees of different Marian shrines, are all evidence of the extent to which evil influences have deflected the impact of the Medjugorje messages on the Church and the wider world. Indeed, the existence of conflict in an apostolic movement which seeks above all to be concerned with peace demonstrates very clearly that Medjugorje is about peace through spiritual warfare, not by organizational means or simply by ignoring the forces of evil. The means selected by Mary are the powers of the Spirit, and where these are deployed so will the contrary forces be in evidence.

Modern rationality, with its sense of civilization as having overcome superstition, inhibits discussion about the existence of powers for evil. It is tolerated in western society to have a belief in God, provided that the implications of this belief are not taken too literally, but it is widely regarded as strange to have any convictions about the existence of an *evil* power. The result of this state of mind in modern secular society is that evil gains power. What we try to explain as social problems, political conflicts, or mental illnesses, need to be looked at more closely. What is going on? The believer wants to know why the plan of God has broken down, why we seem constantly to fall short and go astray in our vocation as the people of God. The answer Jesus gave, the one that modern secular society cannot bring itself to accept, is that his kingdom is not of this world – a world ruled by powers of darkness that are having their hour. Christian life is a struggle against such powers until they are finally nullified by the victory of the cross.

71

Part of the reality of evil is that it conceals itself. We are misled if we assume that because we have not directly encountered evil spirits they cannot exist. How else can we explain the fact that, in spite of all its wonderful powers, talents and virtues, humanity has brought the world to the brink of catastrophe, set upon self-destruction and corrupted in so many ways through individual and social sin? The misuse of body and mind, lovelessness, cynicism and contempt between people, and political oppression and violence, speak not of a rational, humane or holy work, but of a distorted, cursed, obsessed and self-destructive spirit. How could people kill each other if there were no power of evil? How could children be abused or families split? How could there be wars, torture, genocide, ecological destruction and exploitation of poor nations, if our nature was incorrupt? Today we find ourselves polarized as never before, with humanity coming to a frightening clash of values in which there can be no compromise: godless rationalism against paying the vow to God. One position ignores God, while the other pays him tribute and awaits his relief. Neither side can have empathy with the other, because to understand would be to be converted. Christians cannot therefore be surprised if those who most implacably oppose them do so with fierce hatred and disrespect, because that is the nature of evil powers confronted by the evidence of their error.

Modern idols

Opposition to spiritual phenomena also comes from those who, by the way they live their lives, put their faith and hope primarily in material things including wealth and other worldly advantages. With regard to Medjugorje, such opposition is rather to the content than to the fact of the apparitions and messages. Indeed, many of us who accept their authenticity must acknowledge that we resist their implications for our lives because of materialistic concerns. From such resistance develops the direct countering of prophetic truth through sinfulness. This is the consequence to be observed in those modern lifestyles that effectively repudiate any spiritual truth. The ultimate truth is then nothing more than materialistic individualism of the kind that has asserted itself in many western societies today – a puny but cruel philosophy which is gradually being applied to more and more areas of life.

Paradoxically, in their acceptance of individual responsibility, there is a sense in which Christians can accept and transform this credo. They acknowledge that they are allowed by God to be their own judges, and that it is a form of individual freedom, holiness, that permits them to choose to subject themselves, willingly and wittingly, to the absolute truth. If, however, we come to accept spiritual truths, we have to reappraise the material ones which have influenced us, and this means a change of life. For many, the lure of the world is too great. Love of money, of power, of food and drink, of social and intellectual status, or of pleasure, have many so strongly in their grip that they cannot face up to a spiritual judgement, whether this comes from traditional religious authorities or through prophetic messages such as those of Medjugorje. Where people are seduced by worldly values they work at justifying themselves, and this means pushing spiritual and religious concerns to the margins. Even believers are apt to disguise their faith out of deference to the world. The media impose a virtually unquestionable reasonableness, one which would allow any kind of personal ethics, at least in such areas as relationships, enterprise, pleasure-seeking or lifestyle. There is a hardening of hearts, together with the idolizing of the gods of possession and rationalism, which are seen as much more acceptable to worship than a God of love. Mary confronts these idols directly in her messages, as the gospel does.

The gospel offers us paradoxes which can make us wince as their truth bites. For example, we are told by Jesus: 'For anyone who wants to save his life will lose it . . .' (Matthew 16:25), and 'If anyone wants to be first, he must make himself last of all and servant of all' (Mark 9:35). Praying to his

Father, Jesus says: 'I bless you . . . for hiding these things from the learned and the clever and revealing them to mere children' (Luke 10:21), and on the same theme he tells us: '. . . I have come into this world so that those without sight may see, and those with sight turn blind . . .' (John 9:39). We can easily enough see how Jesus is repudiating the values and standards of the world. For worldly honours, people are willing to turn from God, to ignore the promptings of their consciences so as to enjoy the immediate glory and gratifications of career, power, luxury, sensuality, and the lulling of all hurts, doubts and discords in a false peace. 'For what is thought highly of by men is loathsome in the sight of God' (Luke 16:15), because it denies him. And yet God continues to want our conversion and not our destruction. No one is so far from him that they cannot turn back. Somehow God leaves us the choice, however much he may prompt, help or guide us, so that the heart turning to God will be a real conversion.

We have all to some degree chosen what was thought highly of by secular society rather than what God willed. Our very lives attest this. By living in inequality of wealth, and in fragmented families, communities, faiths and nations, we indicate the choices that we have made. Humanity is always tempted to erect its own idols. So it is that we find today's society rich in God's blessing yet preferring to give its homage to its own concerns and creations, such as scientific discoveries, technological applications, superstate power, rights to choose and experiment in biomedical areas, and judgements made daily in the media, the courts and elsewhere that assume humanity's independent capability to find truth.

This view is widely resisted because it flies in the face of many everyday assumptions, and seems to threaten to undo so much apparent good that has actually been achieved in the world. But the nature of modern idolatry is one that takes advantage of our susceptibilities and our blindnesses. The things that we value in the world are not bad in themselves, for example our material possessions, intellectual brilliance, sexuality, and so forth; it is in making a god out of some such element that we blind ourselves, wander off the path, and risk losing all direction. Money provides a good example. Although it serves all kinds of valuable purposes for humanity, it is self-evidently wrong when money is turned into a commodity to be bought and sold and, for example, usurious practices come to defeat all efforts by poor nations to achieve a higher level of education, health and well-being for their citizens. Money can become a god, one that demands true worship, one that wants slaves not subjects, and has its own justification and morality in which profit is truth and prosperity is godly favour.

The idolizing or wanting of anything to excess is a form of greed, the instinct to take for oneself rather than to offer, to share, or simply to leave. Whatever its psychological origins, greed involves our exaggerating our own needs at the expense of someone else. Greed thus destroys our integrity, by causing us to be preoccupied or obsessed by things that constantly falsify our stances in life, for where there is greed there must be pretence, self-deceit, rationalizing, blaming and injustice. Whether the matter is power, money, food, or another scarce good, the game is not played straight. Instead of negotiation and sharing, there is deception, subterfuge, hypocrisy and dishonesty. Lack of probity is a disease that gains on us like a cancer. Relationships are poisoned in families, among friends and work associates, and in all communities that depend upon mutuality, trust and service. The closer we come to acknowledging the truth given to us by the Spirit of God, the more apparent will the powers of evil be that prompt us to idolatry and to resisting the gospel.

Medjugorje and gospel truth

As we look at the work accomplished during his lifetime by Jesus, there is the sense that it appears very much a failure at the time of his death. Not only had the authorities taken action to stamp out the new teaching he was promoting by executing him, but they seemed to have succeeded in their ultimate objective of scattering his followers. Jesus no doubt knew that he would be left alone to undergo his crucifixion, but he had none the less to suffer the pain of abandonment by those with whom he had been working for three years. The Christian mission has always shown these characteristics of a cyclical process of apparently catastrophic failure and unpredicted growth. As it was for the early Church, so it was during the later Roman Empire, and in other times of persecution up to the present day. The gospel has had to be rediscovered so that a new way forward could be found, and its universal truths applied to the ever-changing world of human experience and history. This renewal of the Church and of Christian life is one of the mysteries of faith. Are we seeing another of these moments of rediscovery with the gospel challenge being dramatically proclaimed in Medjugorje at a time when materialism and scepticism have become so widespread?

Fundamental to this challenge is the principle that in the world of the spirit a revolution is needed. For as long as we try to see things simply from a human viewpoint we can only see human visions. To know what God intends is to see another vision. It is to part company with those who make humanity the centre of reality, and to make God central instead. This means envisioning a spiritual reality that is distinct and true in itself, owing nothing to human understanding or intention. This *transcendent* reality is not an answer to humanity, but a question. It calls us to account. It takes us into another sphere of existence and requires of us an openness to what lies beyond, to a realm of contemplation, of awed reverence for God's power and humble acceptance of his love.

Faced by this new reality, what existed before is to be written down as loss, as St Paul says (Philippians 3:7), because it has for long blocked the vision of the transcendent. Now there is knowledge of Jesus both in his incarnate being and in his transcendent nature. It is not that mundane reality is evil, but it is easy for believers to be misled by immanentist perspectives, for example, in the more radical interpretations of liberation theology. God undoubtedly intended that we should serve one another in the material world, but our work also has another dimension of meaning. In themselves, our undertakings are limited, and can have only infinitesimal status in relation to God's transcendent reality. Our glory stems from our being made in the image of God, not from the extent to which we have been able to haul ourselves up to the stature of demigods. God's purposes are being served in every life, prominent or obscure, just as they were served by the hidden life of Jesus' family in Nazareth.

The Virgin Mary repeats to us over and over again that a renewal of Christian life is needed now in the world, and for the world. We have lived a century of despair, of wandering in the desert, alienated from God and from each other. Our accomplishments mean little, because we cannot answer any of the questions that we have about their significance. Where are they leading? What are they for? What can we agree on? What will happen to us? Naturally, into this chaos come many who bring messages about new directions. Either they try to revive something out of the past or they try to sweep away everything that has gone before and ask us to set a new course. These nine-day wonders, from communism to the new sects and cults, offer only false panaceas. The true message has been preached once and for all. We have only to hear it and live it. We are free to say yes or no to God. Our world offers us a thousand ways of saying 'no'. How are we going to be persuaded not to listen to these worldly messages, but instead to say 'yes'?

The reality of Medjugorje, and of Mary's messages, is of the strong intervention by the Holy Spirit which re-poses the question of faith and urges us to respond, promises us the strength to do so, shows us the way it can actually be done in our world, gives us a model of Christian living in the parish of Medjugorje, invites us to come and see, instructs us on what we can do to change our lives by emphasizing the need for prayer and penance, calls us to conversion, and invites us to engage in a work of peacemaking that must begin in our own hearts. The faith to be ignited by the coming new Pentecost in our world will be all the greater because those who experience it will be those who have previously walked in the darkness of rationalist doubt, worldly scepticism, scoffing nonchalance, or fascination with evil. Whatever their state of mind, they did not believe, or they could not believe. And Mary tells us that we are not all to be shown the signs and wonders of Medjugorje. 'Let those who have not seen believe as if they had seen.' That is exactly what Jesus said to the doubting apostle: 'Happy are those who have not seen and yet believe' (John 20:29). If belief is so uncertain, will God really reject those who do not turn to him? On the other hand, if God does exist, all creation must be subject to him, with no exceptions. I cannot adapt creation to suit my whims. It is there, and I have either to believe in God and try as best I can to follow his will, or I have to acknowledge that I am not a believer, and therefore I can do what I like regardless of the consequences – because there can be no *consequences*, in the sense of some ultimate judgement on my actions. When faced with such a clear choice, how can I be sure of myself? The choice has somehow to be made: God and his will, or nothing. In our own power we cannot make such a radical commitment, yet Mary constantly urges us to surrender our lives to God. This can only be done by renewing our faith and hope each day in prayer.

A verdict on Medjugorje

From what must now be hundreds of personal encounters it is my impression that very few who have visited Medjugorje, and prayed there, appear to doubt that events of a supernatural character have been occurring. I personally feel a deep gratitude that this has been my own experience. And yet there are others, both inside and outside of the Church, who deny such claims, who can find no place for them in their vision of reality. Such doubters must then provide a convincing alternative explanation for what is happening to the villagers and the pilgrims, but they have not been able to do so. I feel sure that most of the people I have met through my interest in Medjugorje share a conviction that the Catholic Church will eventually give its endorsement to the supernatural character of the events. When it does, Medjugorje, which is already a world pilgrimage centre, seems destined to extend its influence beyond the Catholic Church, and to become a focus for Christian renewal, through spiritual conversion and the increase of faith and prayer.

People protest that the Medjugorje messages are too difficult to live up to. They say that the spiritual demands made by the Virgin Mary are greater than those conventionally made in the Church today. That is, in matters of prayer, fasting, holiness, and lack of compromise with the secular world, the commitment implied by Mary's messages is total. For some, this is a proof of authenticity, because they see that the world has become a trap for them, and this is the powerful way out, the way to salvation. For others, whose concern is more to relieve than to endure suffering, there is a fear that they are unable to respond, that this challenge is too much and perhaps suspect, the work of enthusiasts who are exaggerating. The question remains, however, for each individual conscience: how much change is involved in being converted? Is the conventional Christianity of the western world a sufficient response, or have we no guarantee of finding salvation by following the majority of those around us? We are told by Mary that the western world has turned away from God. The Church is guided by the Holy Spirit, but this does not mean that it has not been strongly influenced by the world, and thus may no longer be collectively generating the degree of spiritual leadership that God desires.

Why has the Virgin Mary come? Just for the benefit of a small parish in Yugoslavia, or for a few enthusiasts? Are we not going to take her appeals seriously and believe that she bears a message for all of us? How can we know? The only conceivable answer to such questions is that the Spirit will enlighten us, in so far as we seek to live the gospel content of Mary's messages by prayer, penance and holiness of life. We are finding the way to a new purification of the Church. Despite the natural human difficulty of crediting the events and messages of the *Gospa* of Medjugorje, her purity and her love, which are expressed through her very presence and through the messages, can already be seen to be overcoming opposition, whether of disbelief or of evil. However, to believe is not enough. It is conversion of life that is asked for, and an ever-growing commitment to the truth of the gospel. What implications does Mary's presence in Medjugorje have for our doubting, troubled western world? This question is the concern of the remainder of this book.

7

Hope for the Future: a Meditation

Our times need hope, and hope is the very essence of the messages of Medjugorje. Many have come to believe that these messages have been divinely inspired to enlighten the Church and the world today, in line with the gospel-calling to be faithful to God and to collaborate in his creative and redemptive work. Jesus said: 'My Father goes on working, and so do I' (John 5:17). The issue for Christians, or for anyone who wishes to obey the commandments of God, is always to know his will and to trust that knowledge by living in faith. The Virgin Mary's messages in Medjugorje are an encouragement to the Church and for all who will listen to them, because, as she tells us in her eighth anniversary message: 'This is a time of graces' (25/6/1989). We are being offered help to understand more trustingly what God is asking of us in the circumstances of our lives today.

Pope John Paul II has drawn attention to the last decade of this century as a 'new Advent'. He sees the third millennium as promising a new era of faith, just as the birth of Jesus did 2,000 years ago. A major practical programme that he has supported is 'Evangelization 2000', which is planning evangelizing activity throughout the world to coincide with the 'Advent' decade. Such initiatives are quite unlike the missionary endeavours of past centuries. Those most needing to hear the good news of the gospel today are in formerly Christian countries. The need is for the re-evangelization of Europe, West and East, to bring about the spiritual rebirth of whole peoples that have turned away from faith in God. As Pope John Paul has written, 'Contemporary Europe needs to be given a soul and a new self-awareness' (Pope John Paul II, 1986). The work needed is not so much to reject as to reinterpret modern culture in its spiritual origins and dimensions. This rebirth is exactly what the Virgin Mary is calling for in Medjugorje, and she keeps repeating to us that it can only come about through much prayer and penance. Indeed, the re-emergence of Christianity that we have been witnessing in the Soviet Union and throughout Eastern Europe after several decades of persecution can be due to nothing else.

Hope is a spiritual quality. We need to have grounds for hope, but the only possible ground is faith. That is, we possess the future only as a possibility, the realization of which depends to a greater or lesser extent upon factors other than ourselves. Reckoning by human intelligence, even though there is a chance factor or a degree of dependence upon other people in how the future works out, we are driven back largely to a reliance upon our own efforts. Yet we know these to be extremely limited, whatever the degree of confidence we possess in given fields of activity, and at particular moments. Hope can only truly exist for the believer in a loving God. We may mask this from ourselves but there is no other source. This is because our hope is not satisfied by arbitrary developments or substitutes. It has an object of which we are more or less clearly aware, and that is our *need*. Only a power that recognizes our need can meet it. If we set out in anxiety we keep finding that our anxiety is justified. Things do not meet our expectations. But if we set out in hope, Providence takes a hand. God does not ask us to be self-sufficient. We are created beings for whom he is the Provider. Once we have recognized this we can go forward with hope. That is, we can trust God more than we can trust ourselves:

> Be a witness through your life . . . do not worry about anything. If you pray, Satan cannot hinder you even in the least, because you are God's children and he keeps an eye on you. Pray! (message of 25 February 1988)

The prophet is concerned with the here-and-now as well as with the future, but the greater truth is that the kingdom of

God is being built in the here-and-now, and that all other things will pass away. Our hope is constantly referred by the prophets to a God who controls our destinies and is worthy of complete trust. The main questions underlying this chapter are therefore why it is that prophets are often ignored, and why the Medjugorje message can be said to be the prophecy that we most need to hear at the present time. The world today is little different from that of previous generations who have not heard God's messengers: 'Hear and hear again, but do not understand; see and see again, but do not perceive' (Isaiah 6:9). Now, once more, we have a message being proclaimed that will reveal God's plan, both for our lives individually and for the world, but the modern world, even more than past eras, has rejected the notion of a transcendent God, a God who can manifest himself in supernatural events or intervene in human affairs. Such a God is necessarily beyond our knowledge and control, and so has become unimaginable for many. An apparently irresoluble situation results: God offers a message of extreme relevance to humanity, and humanity rejects the possibility of there being such a message.

The reality of God

If we take as a scriptural affirmation of the reality of God 'eternal life is this: to know you, the only true God, and Jesus Christ whom you have sent' (John 17:3), the message is uncompromising, absolute and completely independent of everyday social and political realities. In other words, it is valid for everyone and for every circumstance. What it actually means for a specific situation lived by a particular person has of course to be worked out, by reference to Jesus the incarnate God. That is to say, Jesus reveals to us in his own life a way of being that uses the elements of everyday human existence to find the truth and to glorify God. But the truth to be found depends upon another reality which we cannot know by human wisdom. According to the gospel, and the messages of Mary in Medjugorje, what counts first is the

83

kingdom of God, and therefore the spiritual life, or the relationship between God and humanity. Thus, Jesus on the cross can be understood simply to be dying a noble human death, one to which he has come out of love, humility and obedience, but the greater, *transcendent* reality is that through his death the whole of humanity is being reconciled to the Father. This greater reality can only be known by faith.

I have spoken to people who say that the messages of Medjugorje are not helpful to them because they are too pious, too concerned with personal spirituality, too oblivious of the wider world's problems, weaknesses and needs, and too dismissive of everything that humanity has learnt through its own conscientious procedures of inquiry and reflection. Those who take this view focus their attention upon the immanent reality of relationships between people rather than upon the mysterious, transcendent relationship between people and God. The presentation of the Christian faith that is perhaps most often found in contemporary writing emphasizes such an opening-out to each other, and can appear to imply that the existence or not of an eternal God makes no practical difference to what it would mean to be a good human being.

There is no clear answer as to how we should live, whether the immanentist approach is sufficient for salvation, or whether a transcendental approach will more surely bring us to holiness. Thus, when the lawyer asked Jesus what he needed in order to have eternal life, Jesus told him the story of the Good Samaritan to illustrate that we can love God by loving our neighbour. The immanent and the transcendent closely overlap. The two great commandments, to love God and to love our neighbour, are in many human circumstances one and the same. We are neighbours when we act in a neighbourly way. When we act as neighbours we show love for Jesus. And to love Jesus is to love the Father.

Can we then leave the poor to look after themselves while we concentrate upon spiritual matters? The answer must be no. And can we devote ourselves to the needy, certain that God will notice us even though we are not consciously looking for him? Again, the answer must be no. It is in the end only our own consciences that can tell us how to balance our lives between faith and works of charity. The messages of Mary in Medjugorje reflect how she dealt with this spiritual problem, and they can therefore illuminate us. The human ordinariness of Mary's own life as recounted in the gospels was the occasion for the proclamation of God's majesty, for example when she visited her cousin Elizabeth, and was inspired to utter the Magnificat of the poor people of God.

What is Mary doing now in Medjugorje but repeating that visit, this time to bring the same blessing upon *our* ordinariness? She is guiding us through her motherly qualities of love, interest, gentleness, patient insistence, intensity of feelings and even-handedness, but at the same time she is teaching us to recognize the greatness of God through her own clear vision of him. The lesson must be that only a creature who sees her own nothingness more clearly than we can see ours is able to attain such purity in her gaze upon the Lord, whether in the manger or upon the cross. It is this vision, however, that she wants to share with us through her presence, to help us prepare more trustingly for the coming of Jesus in glory.

The messages of Medjugorje tell us of the same God of mercy and faithfulness, of justice and wisdom, as the psalms and the gospels. It is Jesus, the *one who saves*, who, through his life, death and resurrection, offers us the possibility of reaching out to God from within the compass of our earthly existence. Although his being and attributes transcend our world, they also belong within it. When Jesus explained the Scriptures to the two disciples on the road to Emmaus, and set their hearts on fire, he plainly told them that the prophets had come to foretell the manner of his life and death (Luke 24). This was their purpose. They were to announce to the Jewish people what kind of a Messiah they could expect. They explained why the Messiah would have to suffer, and why the sacrifice of his life would be necessary to atone for sin.

Mary shows us this same Jesus and calls on us to abandon our lives to him, just as he abandoned his life for our

85

redemption. She reminds us that, although we cannot suffer as he did, we can accompany him in his passion in such a way that our sufferings, even a day's fast, can be given a meaning and a value that stem from his sacrifice, not from ourselves. One of the most powerful elements of the Medjugorje apparitions has been the sadness so often expressed to the visionaries by Mary. She is sad because of sin, and because of the suffering that sin has brought upon her son. The only response that we can have to her sadness is sorrow for our sins. Many today want to eliminate repentance, because they see it as the result of a conditioning to guilt by oppressive social structures, among which they number families and the Church. But this is an error of a psychological theory that is not open to the transcendent. We were told 'the kingdom of God is close at hand. Repent' (Mark 1:15). In other words, we *need* repentance to be able to welcome the kingdom. If we cannot see that we really are sinners, or if we are not sorry for our sins, we are not ready for the kingdom.

Sorrow is a grace that we all need. When we feel sorrow we are in effect longing for a transformation, either of ourselves or of the world around us. Helplessly, we want things otherwise, or we wish for the undoing of the effects of the past, or for some way to make up for the evil for which we have been responsible in the past. This is not mere guilt or shame, which can be paralysing, and which springs in any case from pride, but a loving feeling of recognition of our own or others' transgressions, weaknesses and mistakes. That is, when we are sorry, we are taking on the role of the one to whom suffering is caused, and thus are disposing ourselves to seek pardon. Jesus and Mary felt sorrow during the passion on account of all the evils of sin which they both wished to undo through sacrifice, Jesus by his crucifixion and Mary by her unconditional sharing in her son's suffering.

What Mary shows us is that, although we cannot undo the past and make our sorrow unnecessary, we can seek to counterbalance our own or others' faults by our conversion to Jesus. Sorrow provides the energy behind conversion. It prompts us to struggle against evil in ourselves and around us, to become peacemakers, and to be ready to forgive others who are sinners like ourselves. By sorrow we come to respond to evil as Jesus does. He wants all things new. He wants peace and reconciliation. He loves us, and wants us to love one another. And he goes further. He denies our faults: 'Father, forgive them, they do not know what they are doing' (Luke 23:34).

The spiritual dimension to life

Never before in human history as in today's western world have so many people lived in such material comfort, with such opportunities available to them, such services for education, health and welfare, and so little at the mercy of famine, disasters, or wars. Never have people enjoyed so much time for themselves, so much information, knowledge, contacts and variety of communication. Yet it seems that it is in those parts of the world where these conditions are most evident that there is the greatest unbelief. Material and social comforts appear to obstruct the recognition of the spiritual dimension to life.

Yet so many in the West have known a Christian upbringing or have seen believing and practising Christians around them. They have known the story of Christianity down the ages, have watched at close hand the modern desertion of the Church, and may even have participated in it themselves. Such people, and I count myself among them, may themselves have sought meaning in other philosophies and practices, and come to a dead-end. What can then be asked of God other than that he should show us a path which it was once planned that we should tread? We need the light if we are to go on and to avoid turning in circles. There can be no regrets about what we may have missed through past decisions. It has all been gain, provided that we do not stop but continue our journey to its destination. God's will for us is like a tide that will sweep us on to salvation provided we let go of the rocks on which we have allowed ourselves to be spiritually shipwrecked.

Many people are beginning to look at the spiritual dimension to life in ways that are different from how they have ever understood it before (Plunkett, 1990). Modern society offers us material and technological means to satisfy our needs, but there is little evidence that these provide ultimate satisfaction or contentment. A remedy for every illness, a gimmick to deal with every inconvenience, superficial advice to solve every problem, and what is left? More problems than before, and a helter-skelter to try to cope with them. But the spiritual view of life is one that can judge the value of everything (1 Corinthians 2:15), which is to say that the spiritual person has the insight needed to give things their true significance, not their significance within a narrow focus of materialism or self-interest.

Such insight may stem from suffering, from illness, or from a setback in life such as a time of unemployment. Most of the time we are simply too locked into a routine to be able to spare the time to reflect, or to listen to the people who might tell us that things were otherwise and help us to learn something of benefit to our inner, as opposed to our outer and material selves. But what could this insight be? Is there a truth, and could such a truth come from something as familiar as Christianity, something which so many have already rejected and look like refusing for all time to come? We have seen Christianity go through phases of reinterpretation, demythologizing and secularizing, and we have seen alternatives advocated as more progressive, more liberal, or more effective. And yet we live in a world where people continue to feel weighed down by problems, and where there is a growing curiosity about the spiritual. We see people, especially in third-world countries, turning again to religious practices and solutions, and to a belief in the supernatural and its power. Can secular western society once more come to terms with the validity of Christian revelation and with the figure of Jesus as the way, the truth and the life?

Holiness in a secular society seems an unattractive prospect, a denial of much that occupies the minds and hearts of people. Holiness is seen as antiquated and uninteresting. It appears to refuse the variety of human experience in order to be subjected to external authority in joyless self-denial and opting out. Because of the prevalence of such thinking it is easy for Christian believers to feel discouraged and isolated, or to feel divided in their loyalties. The material world beckons them alluringly, and they are strongly tempted to strike a compromise. It seems unlikely that anyone will make much progress towards holiness if they begin by looking at its cost. Holiness cannot be a project for the worldly, but only for those who have decided to put the kingdom of God first. Holiness means being filled with the presence of God, being complete, whole, reconciled, renewed, healed, innocent, and at one with God; and simultaneously joyful and at peace in this knowledge. The context can never be some kind of *bargain* we strike with God about what we are going to retain and what we are going to surrender.

Spiritual transformation will come about as the fruit of creation being directed towards the fulfilling of God's will. This implies our developing a unity of mind and purpose throughout the world, the sharing of our planet through an attitude of respect for 'the integrity of creation', and the recognition of the presence of God in each created being and situation. The practical consequences of this are the tasks of dissolving obstacles to wholeness and holiness, removing human barriers, bringing strength to each other and finding peace. And this work can only be undertaken by being referred to God in faith – not by our seeking to take over God's creative role but by our being open to his renewing Spirit. Worry comes from assuming total responsibility where the problem is beyond us. If we abandon our concern, acknowledging that we do not and cannot know the future, then the way is open for it to be dealt with by God. I am struck by the prayer which says that the Spirit 'holds all things together and knows every word spoken by man'. We cannot invite the Spirit into our lives on our terms. We are known completely. It is the Spirit who has the initiative.

Thus, all the good things that people do, all the beautiful thoughts and words they conceive, are born in them through the Holy Spirit, just as Jesus was conceived in Mary. We do not have the love, knowledge and wisdom to predict the Spirit, even though we know that it is in consistency with those virtues that the Spirit always acts.

The world therefore has sooner or later to acknowledge the Spirit as gift, as hope for the future. Our attempts to be independent of the Spirit are doomed to failure. It is only by turning to the Spirit in prayer that we can transform our human strivings. What we can hope for from the Spirit are sincere and open hearts, a knowledge of truth, and a growing willingness to serve God and our neighbour. Everything seems poised in our world for a strong coming of the Holy Spirit. He is needed now as he was at Pentecost, and this is why Pope John XXIII prayed for a new Pentecost when he opened the Second Vatican Council in 1962. The new life that the Spirit brings is not something obscure of which we will hardly be aware. It will involve a transformation of our everyday ways of seeing, feeling and thinking. We will be enabled to look at the truth that lies beneath appearances. Instead of being captivated by the world, that very world can benefit from our love. We can be a source of love, and thus come to look afresh upon the people around us, seen now in the image of Jesus. The understanding of this process, in which we are involved at the present moment and at every moment of our lives, comes to us through the wisdom of the Holy Spirit. We are led to see the true and the good rather than be victims to falsity in ideas, circumstances and relationships. We are in fact set free from what has bound us so that we are available for a new way of being. In essence, this new way of being is to understand our existence as God-given, as having a plan, as dignifying us and all people with a destiny that transcends our present existence.

The Scriptures are full of metaphors for rebirth and new life. The Exodus is an archetype of these, but the New Testament offers many more, such as the new covenant, baptism, living water, salvation and the kingdom. And we are called to this new life. While *renewal* is a term currently used to refer to the process of Christians coming to recognize the power of the Holy Spirit, it would be a misconception to see any particular group as monopolizing such an experience. Just as each day we can begin our pilgrimage towards God, so the Spirit is continually coming to us in response to our prayers to 'renew the face of the earth'. But the special recognition of the Spirit in our times in the Church is a great grace for a world that has wandered along paths leading away from God. We can confidently await the moment when we will get a sense of the world turning again, under the guidance of the Holy Spirit and through the prayerful intercession of the Virgin Mother of God, to set out on a new path towards God. 'The Spirit and the Bride say: "Come!" ' (Revelation 22:17; and see the book of the same title by Farrell and Kosicki, 1981). What a great new Exodus that will be, when humanity escapes from the reign of sin and darkness to a new life of love and peace! The renewal prefigures the kingdom and constitutes a challenge to Christians to reach out towards others, to encourage them to welcome a renewed spiritual life. Every day can bring conversion, a trustful step forward into new life and new situations, as well as into trials and expressions of faith and love.

Messages still to come

It is only through confidence in the Holy Spirit that we can feel reconciled to the Medjugorje messages that relate to the future. Many have said that they dislike the notion of the Virgin Mary holding 'secrets' about the future over us like a sword of Damocles. But in fact she has only ever given messages of hope and faith, an inspiration we can expect to continue to receive in the future. In a message to Mirjana on 18 March 1989, Mary spoke about the future and said specifically that she does not wish to threaten so much as to 'beseech' us 'to pray, to help her by our prayer for unbelievers' (Mirjana's account, dated 19/3/89). The messages to come

91

refer, we are told, to events which are *conditional* upon the response to the messages that have already been given. But we already know that the future of the world is in our hands. If we continue to face each other with aggression we will end by destroying each other. We do not know when, but it is sure to happen. Only a change of heart can save us. As Mary says:

> Don't think about wars, chastisements, evil. It is when you concentrate on these things that you are on the way to enter into them. Your responsibility is to accept divine peace. (message to Jelena, *c.* 1983)

Mary has also told the visionaries that a permanent sign will appear at the site of the first apparitions in Medjugorje, that is, on the small hill Podbrdo. Its purpose will be to confirm the authenticity of the apparitions for all who are open to them, but who feel subject to doubt or disbelief.

The visionary, Mirjana, has been entrusted with knowledge of certain future events which she will be permitted to notify to a priest of her choice a few days before they are due to occur. In his letter to Pope John Paul II, dated 2 December 1983, Fr Tomislav Vlasic stated:

> Before the visible sign is given to humanity, there will be three warnings to the world. The warnings will be in the form of events on earth. Mirjana will be a witness to them . . . The sign will be given as a testimony to the apparitions and in order to call people back to faith. (O'Carroll, 1986: 210)

We are told that the time will be short, and for some there will be insufficient time, so that we should not casually wait to see before making up our minds whether to take a decision for God. Already in 1983 Mary urged:

> Do not wait for the sign; the sign will come too late for those who do not believe. The only word I want to say is 'conversion' of the whole world!

We can only conclude that once this sequence begins to be

revealed we will face a choice like that described in John's Gospel: 'Anyone who believes in the Son has eternal life, but anyone who refuses to believe in the Son will never see life' (John 3:36).

Although we do not know the times and reasons, it is surely appropriate to reflect on what may be the nature of the gift that God is giving us through the Medjugorje signs for the future. Mary told the visionary Mirjana that all adults are able to know God, and that their unbelief is culpable: 'Every adult has the ability to know God; the sin of the world consists of this – in not searching for God' (Vlasic and Barbaric, 1986: 106). We might indeed expect that God in his infinite love would give everyone the opportunity to know him, though not as a human certainty and not by compulsion. To impose himself would not be consistent with the way that God has always dealt with humanity. We are invited to come to know, love and serve God of our own free will.

The reason why Mary insists that we should look to the future with hope is so that we can begin to make the needed response now:

> The world has forgotten the value of fasting and prayer; with fasting and prayer wars could be stopped and natural laws suspended. (message of 21 July 1982)

This is a special time of grace when we are intended to be preparing ourselves for whatever lies in God's plan. We are not told specifics of that plan, but some things seem patent. There is to be a time when everyone will have to make a choice for or against God. That is, many more than at present will need to look into their own hearts and say whether or not they accept God. Something new will be glimpsed of the implications of this choice: the way of truth and conversion of heart, or the denial of God's claims. The choice will have to be made within time constraints, Mary tells us. God wants to see his reign of light and truth extended throughout creation, and he has decided that the time is now approaching for those who wish to live that way to have the possibility of doing so. There can be no failure of justice on God's part,

93

but some may refuse, or be unwilling to seize the opportunity to acknowledge him and to be converted from atheism and self-centred ways of living. He will not force them. What of believers? The first impact on them will be to challenge them to turn even more whole-heartedly to God, but it will also be their task to seek to persuade those who continue in their refusal to open their hearts to God. This will be a time of urgent and radical witness:

Be strong in God. I desire that through you the whole world will come to know the God of joy. By your life, bear witness to that joy. Do not be anxious or worried. God himself will help you and show you the way. I desire that you love all men with my love only and, by that means, love can reign over the world. (message of 25 May 1988)

Looking further ahead, when we know not what events will have ensued, it may be surmised that there will be a time of very great returning to God in the world. The visionaries have told Father Vlasic that 'people will believe as in ancient times' (Vlasic, 1983). The Holy Spirit will inspire those who are willing to accept God, so that they come easily to belief, but they will need to turn to the Church for an authentication of their apparently personal experience of conversion. The Church will inevitably be challenged as never before to be a teaching Church, an ongoing inspiration to those who are finding God, and who need the spiritual sustenance of worship, teaching, guidance and the ministry of the sacraments. People turning to the Church will need to understand about Medjugorje in the first instance, but this will not be the essence of their search. Once they make the connection between Medjugorje and the gospel of Jesus, they will see that Medjugorje is merely the path to the path. This challenge will be first and foremost to the bishops and priests, who will be called to respond very powerfully. For this, they will need the spiritual support of their people. But the number of Christian leaders will be greatly insufficient, and therefore all Christians will be needed for the task. Existing groups, associations and works of all kinds in the Church will find a new purpose, and will need a new vision.

After the period of frequent and concentrated messages from Medjugorje over the past few years, there has come a period of comparative silence at the time of writing. Mary continues to appear, but we learn little further detail of God's plan centring on Medjugorje to which so many of her earlier messages referred. What can we deduce from this? Surely that this is a time to digest what we have been told, and to be preparing for the next phase which may encompass the revealing of the secrets and their consequences. In his book subtitled *Délai de miséricorde*, René Laurentin explores the idea that this is a time of mercy for people to find their response to whatever God is asking of them. Fr Philip Pavic, of the parish of St James in Medjugorje, has suggested a related idea in his homilies. He sees the times as a *kairos*, not merely a personal opportunity for conversion but a critical moment for humanity collectively. Perhaps the 'delay' can be understood in the sense that St Peter speaks of: 'The Lord is not being slow to carry out his promises . . . but he is being patient with you all, wanting nobody to be lost and everybody to be brought to change his ways' (2 Peter 3:9).

Whatever the future, Mary asks us to prepare for it by prayer, penance, conversion, faith and the building of peace and reconciliation. Time for this is limited, in the sense that we can presume that what has been foretold by Mary will happen within the lifetimes of Mirjana, who is to reveal the secrets before they occur, and Fr Petar Ljubicic, the priest through whom she will make her announcement. But whether this assumption is valid or not, Mary constantly asks us for an immediate decision for God:

> I am again appealing to you today to turn totally towards God – which those find difficult who have not made a decision for him. My appeal, dear children, is that you be wholly converted to God . . . place your life in God's hands. (message of 25 January 1988)

Christians who have listened to Mary and to other prophets

of the Church are therefore not only being called to redouble their efforts spiritually through prayer and surrender of their lives, but also to lay the foundations for a time of mission involving the whole Church for the sake of the salvation of the world. The final chapter of this book will therefore be devoted to an exploration of what this work of preparing for the future might be, in the light of the convergence of the messages of the gospel and those of the *Gospa* of Medjugorje.

8

Three Routes to the Kingdom

Believers in Christ are called to work for his kingdom on earth and in the world to come. That is, their everyday life has both a present value and an eternal significance. How are they to approach this work? In the light of the messages of Medjugorje, the guiding principle is that of peace. Mary desires to have the title Queen of Peace, which parallels Jesus' title of Prince of Peace. The whole spiritual movement of prayer, fasting, conversion and faith, which the Medjugorje messages sustain, is directed to peace. Peace is the point of arrival for the human spirit, for the body of Christ being built in the Church, and it is the state fulfilled in paradise, when all things are made new. The Virgin Mary is showing the way to the kingdom, and is therefore indicating the spiritual means to adopt to be reconciled to God. There is a family of words that recur in her messages, including *reconciliation, atonement, purification, surrender* and *conversion,* that cause pain because they demand that we go back on decisions freely made in the past. Through this pain we find renewal. Each new day brings the possibility of a choice to make the road straight for the Lord, to level all mountainous obstacles and to bridge all isolating gaps. The benefit of this change of heart is to be once more *at peace* with God and with all his creation.

Mary's messages in Medjugorje emphasize that the reconciliation needed for the building of the kingdom demands not only the conversion of unbelievers and sinners but also the coming to completeness of the Church as the united body of Christ and the carrying of peace to the whole of creation. I want to bring this book to a close by concentrating particularly on these three aspects of this broader vision in both their spiritual and temporal dimensions.

Why these three themes? In the first place, there can be little doubt that one of the main obstacles to the building of the kingdom of God is the division among believers. If Christians were truly converted and the Christian Church was united, how could the gospel's persuasive power be resisted? It is the division in the Church that gives unbelievers the excuse to continue to ignore its claims. A second, no less major, feature of our times is the refusal of God, accompanied by the growing influence of evil which is all the more insidious for being vociferously denied by so many who consider themselves among the most educated and the most modern. The need for the light and truth of the gospel is greater than it has ever been, and it is becoming apparent that this very fact is dimly perceived in the world, so that there is a thirst for the unknown God that no human remedies can assuage. And, thirdly, it is undeniable that contemporary society is expert at cataloguing its own needs, so that it is particularly easy for us today to list the ills of hunger, disease, poverty, torture, oppression, violence, war, and all the other distortions of human peace and order that characterize our world. The remedying of such problems is therefore one of the most obvious ways we could take towards God, and yet it will be treated here as the third way to the kingdom, because it seems that we need personal and spiritual healing before we can see our world through God's eyes, as it were, and truly invoke his healing on the whole of creation. As Mary said in her message on Christmas Day 1988:

> My dear children, I call you to peace. Live it in your heart and around you so that everyone may know this peace which does not come from you but from God.

'May they all be one' (*John 17:21*)

Two things that Mary has said concerning the Church should give us pause for thought. The first is that divisions in religion are man-made and that we should respect all faiths, and the second is that the Pope is to be a father to all people, not just to Catholics. Though this could be taken as a Catholic Church-centred view, it is increasingly widely accepted by Christians that there is a need for an office, though not necessarily a hierarchical one, to symbolize and to provide a point of reference for the unity of the Church despite persisting doctrinal differences. Mary tells us that such differences can be resolved, by prayer far more than by discussion, and it is perfectly clear that Pope John Paul II is committed to this view. In fact his whole pastoral action and missionary activity best make sense when viewed in this perspective. Initiatives taken towards Orthodoxy, towards Protestant Churches, Buddhists and others, the world day of prayer at Assisi, the sixty-six references to the Father God in his address to Muslim youth in Morocco, and his references to the Jews as the elder brothers of Christians when meeting the Chief Rabbi of Rome, are all signs that indicate not only the gathering of Christians but the embracing of all faiths and cultures within a common human identity before God.

Although we live in a world in which there are exclusive classes, castes and religious groupings, it is also an age of *rapprochements*, whether through travel and knowledge of foreign cultures, instantaneous television coverage of events around the world, or even through the common fear of the threat from growing numbers of outsiders, such as fanatics, terrorists and people with extremist ideologies. More positively, there is a secular holistic philosophy that shows itself in development work, the green movement, human rights organizations, internationalist groups, cultural exchange programmes, and the like. As far as Christian Churches are concerned, it is clear that there is an ecumenical willingness to cope with denominational differences that appeared as deep gulfs less than twenty years ago. After centuries of effort to see the weaknesses in each other's positions, it is a new experience of many groups to be recognizing each other's strengths, insights and contributions. Realizing that it cannot be Christian to seek to manipulate people into belief or unity, the Churches are developing their strategies for contact with each other, while trusting in God for the eventual outcome. Historical human communities, even ecclesiastical ones, are undoubtedly entitled to a love of their own traditions and to a desire to advocate them. Beyond that they are called to be open collaborators with God's will, and these seem to be times when initiatives on his part can be expected.

'Make disciples of all the nations' (Matthew 28:19)

Jesus came to call all humanity. His teaching was not for certain cultures or regions; in fact it is clear that his message appeals throughout the world. If Christianity has been so powerful in the West in the past, this has not been without consequences for how it has been interpreted and accepted elsewhere. Contemporary Christianity needs to be separated from cultural trappings if its essence is to be available to people from differing cultural traditions. The tendency to teach religion in schools as a cultural study, through the method of comparison, is thus potentially unsound at the spiritual level, for it neglects the core of religion and promotes relativism. No religion, Christian or other, is well served by such treatment. We can, on the other hand, recognize the value of all religions that pursue a fundamental search for truth, for God, and for ways of living that honour and serve God, or at least for a higher purpose than the individual's self-interest. Nor is any one way perfected in practice. However much the adherents of a faith believe in their own truth, they can still learn from other traditions.

In seeking to reach out to non-Christians, and indeed to beyond the sphere of believers in a divine being, Christians are pursuing the desire of Jesus that light should come to all humanity through his gospel: 'Go, therefore, make disciples of all the nations . . . teach them to observe all the commands I gave you' (Matthew 28:19–20). But this binding together of humanity is not an exclusively Christian dogma, so much as a characteristic of the race. It is written into our natures in the bonding of man and woman, the development of family, clan, nation, groups and social organizations. The human sciences are concerned with how such bonding occurs or develops. We see rationally that much depends upon these processes that are so little understood. What Christianity and other world faiths contribute is the insight that it is the *spiritual* bonding that must precede and empower all the other forms.

Ultimately, this leads to the spiritual insight, one that is independent of scientific or rational truth, that we know who we are, and why we exist, inductively, having regard to our spiritual natures. We do not *assert* our individuality, however much contemporary society may assume this; we *receive* it. It is true that we interpret this gift, and that its interpretation is a marvellous adventure, but we need to start from the spiritual. Only by following this approach is it possible to avoid the thankless quest of secular humanism, which is to expand the ego so as to absorb the consciousness of others. And that is not the true nature of things in a universe in which God is the Creator and has made us as unique beings. In theological terms, the relationship of love between Father and Son precedes the creation of the world, and thus all things are to be conformed to this relationship, including the birth, life, death and resurrection of Jesus, the nature and purpose of the Church he founded, and the people who have been called to fit into this pattern to find the meaning of their existence.

The Christian duty to evangelize is made clear in the New Testament, especially in the gospels and the writings of St Paul, and the same emphasis is to be found in Mary's messages in Medjugorje. Moreover, the example of Jesus was to preach to all, while knowing that only some would be converted, and so it follows that evangelizing is passing on the good news not merely to those who are open to it, but even to those who show no signs of being interested. Success, least of all immediate success, is not the test. When St Paul preached in Athens he gave witness seemingly without fruit, even though Greek culture was eventually to make such a great contribution to the development of the Christian world.

The commitment Mary asks is to be faithful to her messages by not distorting them and turning them into our own messages. We live in a time when innumerable varieties of the Christian message have developed, but this cannot be what God wants. We are urged by Mary to seek the truth of the gospel by returning to the reading of Scripture as a daily practice, and by praying the Creed. The Creed, she has said, is her favourite prayer. The essence of the Creed is belief in the reality of the transcendent God: the life of Jesus given for our salvation through the mercy of God the Father and the light of the Holy Spirit. When believers seek to convey this Creed to someone else they are not attempting to prove anything by argument or scholarship, but are helping the other to engage in the familiar exchange between God and his people, where the word of God goes out and does not return without 'succeeding in what it was sent to do' (Isaiah 55:11).

How then does this relate to a world which no longer seems able to hear the words of the Creed or the gospel, either because the message is unwelcome or because the language used to transmit it is regarded as discredited? The temptation for the Christian is to modify the message or the language to find favour, or else to say nothing and simply to hope and pray that the truth of Christianity will convince unbelievers without the spoken message. However, this is not at all the example given by the apostles, either the first time that they were sent out 'and went from village to village proclaiming the good news and healing everywhere' (Luke 9:6), and even less after Pentecost, or by St Paul in Athens. The apostles followed the instruction not to make provision for their journeys, and to trust the Holy Spirit for what they would say. If we think of the world today, it is certain that the instruction is the same: to trust and to be courageous in action. Courage is needed precisely because the kingdom has not yet come, but the opportunities, the words and the fruits will all be given by the Holy Spirit. Once again, the model of Mary is a powerful one, since she gives the greatest example of courage of all God's creatures, sublimely affirming her son at the foot of his cross, at the very moment when everyone, Jew and Gentile alike, was either condemning him or deserting him. Her actions must have been the fruit of much love and prayer, and of a life of profound holiness.

Evangelization is love shared among people, for the good news is of saving love. The word evangelization is a concept, and we should recognize that the evangelists did not know they were *evangelizing*. What they were doing was living the gospel out of love. The promise of Pentecost is that the lost will be saved, not by those armed with argument but by those prepared by the Spirit to speak humbly of the truth and to meet the hunger and thirst of souls. Here we could take the example of St Joseph rising from his sleep and gathering his family for the journey to Egypt without hesitation, in faith and obedience. Egypt is the land of the pharaohs, the province of unbelievers and idolaters. The Christian is to go there when summoned. But of course it may be that there is no actual physical journey, just the acceptance of a new attitude to those around us. Contemporary western society is also a world of sceptics and rationalists, of those who worship alien gods and none, and indeed of thoughtless blasphemy. What Mary is telling us is that this situation is unacceptable to God. The world must not continue to ignore God if, as she tells us, it is possible for every adult to know God. There are also those who actively seek to dismiss the truth, which they see as imprisonment rather than freedom. For unbelievers, uncertainty has its security, because anything is then allowable, and they are free from self-reproach in the enjoyment of their possessions, whether power, material goods, pleasures or reputation.

Where, then, should the work of evangelizing begin? So many groups claim our attention; so many individuals cross our paths. None the less the situation of young people in a virtually pagan modern world is a particularly pressing concern for Christians. Mary has spoken directly about this at

Medjugorje, when she asked for a Year for Youth following the Marian Year (message of 14 August 1988). The young have to some extent been abandoned by the older generation, for so few have had any religious upbringing. They must be in the forefront of the evangelist's concern. Former Christians too, those who no longer acknowledge their origins, are also in special need. Many of them are close to believing, and are living in a vague agnosticism because they have simply lost confidence in all they used to hold to, as a result of the influence of rationalist and materialist society. The Church has a special concern for 'all those who have wandered from their spiritual home', as Pope John Paul said in Sydney in November 1986. And Jesus spoke of going in search of the lost sheep, the one who had gone astray.

It would seem from Mary's messages that she has a special concern for those who are furthest away, those who cause most hurt to themselves and others by the evil in their lives, those abandoned to Satan, even consecrated to Satan. The great work of the Church is the conversion of sinners, for, although we all need the gospel to be preached to us continually, there are times in our lives when we need to be awoken with a start, to be converted or reconverted. In the case of unbelievers whose frame of mind may be that of self-righteousness or contempt for God, the Christian sees their position as founded on error or pretence. In the place of truth they may have put the legitimacy of family claims, the legality of their authority, the influence of their status or money, the ignorance of their enemies or victims, or the hope that their bluff will never be called.

To maintain their position, such unbelievers not only deny the truth but attack, vilify or censor it, while all the while hiding what they are doing. Indeed, our modern world has coined the term 'disinformation' to refer to the construction of lies and false evidence used by those who seek to destroy the truth. As they move further and further away from the truth, they are able to persecute those who represent it by progressively more subtle means. Thus it is undeniable that the oppression of Christian belief and ways of life in secular western society is more effective than it has been in the countries of the eastern bloc. So what are Christians to do? Their options are limited. If they are to be faithful to the truth, they must express it in some way. They can only adjust their message to a limited extent, such as by choosing their moment, words, medium, friends, defence or silence. But in the end they must speak the truth they believe in, and suffer the consequences. It is more important to speak the truth than to save themselves. They are only the messengers. The truth does not depend upon them but upon the one who has sent them.

The potential of the truth is always that it will set us free – and that is the ultimate purpose of the evangelist. This is also why the truth will always be welcomed by some, although it cannot be known beforehand who these will be. The evangelist has to believe that it can be any of those to whom the word is proclaimed. No one should be excluded from being offered the message, not the enemy, not the one who mocks, not the harsh nor the unjust, not even the one who seems serene in unbelief or the one who seems to have all the earthly rewards, because nothing is to be compared with the privilege of knowing Jesus Christ (Philippians 3:8). The evangelist has freely received, and so must freely give.

Again and again Mary urges us not only to live the messages she gives us but to pass them on to others: 'I want you to be active in living and conveying the messages' (5/6/86). It is exactly as Jesus asked: 'Proclaim the good news to all creation' (Mark 16:15). This aspect of Christianity cannot be set aside out of a false respect for the opinions of others, because there is no human opinion that deserves as much respect as God's truth. The fact that there are many who do not hear the word of God because there is no one who dares to speak it to them in a secularized world is a terrible reproach to Christian love in practice. This does not imply that Christians should impose their faith, but that they should freely share their own experience of God, their beliefs and their traditions.

Latin-American liberation theologians speak of poor people

105

in the basic Christian communities 'evangelizing' the Church (Barreiro, 1982: 67), and this provides an important insight. It is not always those who think they possess knowledge of the truth who have understood it best. Sharing the word of God invariably becomes a two-way process. We evangelize each other by human sharing and by supporting each other's faith, as well as by direct teaching. However, even if we do these things, their ultimate effect is up to God. Conversion and belief come only from the Spirit; the Christian's part is to be faithful in prayer and to be open to the gifts and guidance the Spirit gives.

The Virgin Mary comes to Medjugorje to proclaim the good news afresh. The pilgrims are those who heard of her coming and were led to go to see for themselves. Most found much more than they expected, and then wished to share their experience with others. Mary has said that she needs our support in the plan that she is carrying out on God's behalf, especially through our prayer and fasting. She is not doing something *to* us, but for us and with us. As they return home, the pilgrims are finding that they are no longer the same. They have seen the saving work of God in progress. They realize that others need to hear and see what they have heard and seen, and to learn of the peace that so many associate with Medjugorje: a kind of serenity in following God's will as they wait for his plan to unfold, but also a strong desire that others may come to share their faith.

'He has exalted the lowly' (Luke 1:52)

When we attend to what Mary is actually saying in Medjugorje we can find no justification for regarding it as a pious turning of the back upon the troubles of the world to wait for the kingdom to come. It simply is not that kind of spirituality that she proposes. What she does say, however, is that the world has to be changed interiorly as well as exteriorly, and that the interior, spiritual change is primary. In other words, it is as our own hearts change that others will change. 'If you pray in your hearts, dear children, the ice-cold hearts of your brothers and sisters will melt . . .' (23/1/86). It is true that Mary puts prayer and fasting first as remedies for the world, just as she points to the passage from Matthew 6 about trusting in God as the cornerstone of Christian life. But no one can read the psalms, the prophets, the gospels or the epistles and claim that God wants works rather than faith. He wants both, but faith first. 'If Yahweh does not build the house, in vain the masons toil' (Psalm 127).

Mary's messages constantly propose works of charity: giving our work over to the Lord by praying before and after work (5/7/84), engaging in works of charity (5/12/85), loving others (13/12/84; 6/6/85; 29/5/86), giving the light to others (14/3/85), encouraging others to find unity and peace (31/7/86; 25/9/86), and performing good deeds of love and mercy (25/3/87). It is made very clear that the Christian life involves ensuring that the needs of others are met, and this means not only their spiritual, but also their material and social needs. It can therefore be said that there is a third route to the kingdom which is through peace and justice in the world, through the recognition that all are one, that every life is of equal value, that everyone is worthy of unconditional respect, and that we will find our own salvation by living a life of Christian love.

This is the same message as that found in the Magnificat (Luke 1:46–55). The messages of Medjugorje closely reflect Mary's hymn to the glory and mercy of God on behalf of the poor and humble of the earth. What brings peace and justice to the world is faith in God's promises, not human effort alone. The proud and the mighty will be cast aside, the humble will be exalted, and the hungry filled with good things. It is true that her prayer is not a rallying-call for human struggle, since all divisions and conflicts are false to the unity that faith implies, but we can see the Magnificat as a prophetic statement about the raising of consciousness of the people, a message of hope to the suffering, and an encouragement to all who are oppressed. It is impossible to live hopefully and at the same time to condone war, the arms race and injustice, whether these stem from unredeemed violence in people's hearts or from the narcissistic nationalism of world powers. All are called to conversion, even, and indeed especially, those who are already preaching the gospel.

Peace and justice are fundamentally matters of spiritual conversion. In the case of the issue of aid to the poor nations of the world, for example, the modern world appears blind to its injustice. In former times it would not have been in the power of the wealthier areas of the world to help other regions. They did not have the competence. Charity was feasible only *within* communities. But now we have all the resources of information, wealth, communications, technical knowledge and decision-making machinery to make the worldwide sharing of material welfare feasible. The situation therefore in which collectively we continue to allow tens of thousands of people to die from hunger each day, or untold millions to live in a state of chronic hunger, disease and misery, because there is no political pressure to change things compared with the pressure we feel to advance our own welfare, is truly one that cries out to heaven. And perhaps there is a parallel here with the way the unborn are treated. They too are silent, and thus are widely regarded as having no rights. How can we continue to live our lives without giving rights to the unborn, or the poor, the marginalized, the blacks, the handicapped, the unemployed and the hungry? These injustices of the modern world must surely all be one in the eyes of God, and in the perspective on life that the Blessed Virgin offers us.

A further dimension to Mary's messages, similarly consistent with the Magnificat, is that we are a people travelling together towards God. It is not the case that she proposes a spirituality that is solely one of a relationship to the transcendent God. We are also to take his peace to all creation, as has already been recalled. It could be said that we will come to God together or not at all, because the commandment is that we should love God *and* our neighbour; and our neighbour is everyone. The teaching of the Good Samaritan parable has made this irrevocably clear. A protest movement which addresses causes, but not our neighbours' needs, will not serve. When we stopped to tend a neighbour, did we do it to deal with a case, to demonstrate our concern to others, to accuse someone else, or was it out of respect for the person's humanity and eternal destiny? Did we see Jesus in them? This is the gospel, and it is this message of peace and justice that the Magnificat and the words of Mary in Medjugorje are recalling.

'Set your hearts on his kingdom first' (Matthew 6:33)

We approach the kingdom with so many gospel comparisons in our minds, so many strands of thought, that we might be tempted to try to simplify them, to look for a kingdom that can be understood, identified, or demonstrated. It is true that we are building the kingdom when we help others in need, bring an end to injustice and conflict, become reconciled to God in our hearts, or pass on to others the good news of redemption. But these can only be aspects of the kingdom. Jesus did not offer us one single statement about the kingdom; instead he left us a rather bewildering series of images and other statements which create an impression of variety or elusiveness. It must be true that the kingdom is within, that is, within our grasp, that it is not of this world, that it is like a mustard-seed, a new Jerusalem, a harvest, a great banquet, and many other things besides, for this is what Jesus taught, and it is for all this that we pray when we say: 'Thy kingdom come.'

Mary, the Queen of Prophets, is opening our eyes to this vision. She says: 'Make paradise your goal' (25/10/87), but she also tells us that it is by leading our ordinary lives according to God's will that we can be worthy of heaven. The paradox of God's majesty and our lowliness, however important we may rank in human terms, is that we earn nothing. All is gift, even to the most industrious, zealous or productive. Once again, this is the message of the Magnificat: 'He has looked upon his lowly handmaid' (Luke 2:48). If Mary acknowledged her lowliness and servant status, which of us can make any claim or assumption that the kingdom can be built other than the way God planned it? And is there any way to know what God's plan for the world is, and to become a participant in the building of his kingdom, other than through the means Mary proposes to us of prayer, penance, conversion, faith and peaceful reconciliation?

Human life is a journey extending beyond space and time. We know this naturally through our powers of imagination, memory and reason. It is therefore self-evident that our destination cannot be glimpsed in socio-political terms. We only know our ultimate destiny as prophecy, in hope, recognizing that the goodness of God is more thoroughly reliable than any human possibility. God and his saints in glory, eschatological peace in the new Jerusalem, are objects of wonder and praise, not of human calculation. The truth of the cross, exemplified so majestically by Krizevac in Medjugorje, and its victory in the resurrection, cannot be set aside. This was Christ's way, lived in obedience, and it will be the way of all who set their hearts on the kingdom first. For some this means human suffering, for others long years of work for peace and justice in the world, but for all it means acceptance of salvation as a gift, in an indispensable inner stillness of worship, like the state of Mary's soul as she prayed just before the angel came to announce that the Redeemer would be born.

Epilogue

It was the intention of this book simply to offer one person's understanding of the spiritual message of Medjugorje. My underlying conviction has been that God has permitted the Virgin Mary to speak as a prophet to the world at a time of grave need. Particularly in the western world, materialism and secularism have dimmed faith to such an extent that even those who claim to be Christians often look first to natural solutions for problems of meaning and for the way forward in the everyday difficulties of life. Over against this, Mary reminds us of the Gospel of Matthew, in which we are advised to trust God for everything. Her spiritual teaching expands this basic gospel message.

The book has sought to show how Mary's role as prophet stems from Scripture, especially from the words she herself spoke in the Magnificat, how it has been accepted and celebrated by some of the main traditions of the Christian Church, and how her purpose has been communicated to us through the young visionaries of Medjugorje. The authenticity of the apparitions and messages of Medjugorje cannot be proved, but their effects in people's lives can be observed. I admit to the privilege of having known a considerable number of people whose lives have been changed through the impact of the spiritual message of Medjugorje. This has made it easier for me to write of my belief and trust in the gospel-based truth to be found in Mary's messages.

The question the book raises, however, is not one of scientific validity, but of faith. The spiritual message of Medjugorje is one that speaks to the heart, not to the mind. If hearts are closed, then there is no message. If, on the other hand, the need is felt for an alternative to the rationalist and materialist purposes of modern society, if a void is sensed when the question of meaning and purpose arises, then a full answer is, I am personally convinced, to be found in the way offered us by the Blessed Virgin.

Writing as a Catholic does not entitle me to speak for the Catholic Church. I believe that the Spirit guides the Church and I shall accept the teaching of the Church on Medjugorje. Therefore, while the events of Medjugorje continue, and though I believe that they will eventually attract the approval of the Church, it is my view that a Christian should exercise due caution in approaching the phenomena of Medjugorje. There is no place for credulity of the kind that can lead to superstition or fatalism. The way must be one of prayer, the opening of the heart to God. If Medjugorje is part of God's purpose, then it will continue to show its fruits in people's lives in so far as they are willing. The question for today, as for all times in which the gospel has been preached, is therefore whether we are willing, in a prayer out of our human weakness, to set aside the obstacles that impede our truly hearing Mary's prophetic message.

Bibliography

Addis, W. E. and Arnold, T. (eds), *A Catholic Dictionary* (Virtue 1954)

Barreiro, A., *Basic Ecclesial Communities: the Evangelization of the Poor* (Orbis, New York 1982)

Brown, R. E., *et al.* (eds), *Mary in the New Testament* (Geoffrey Chapman 1978)

Craig, M., *Spark from Heaven: the Mystery of the Madonna of Medjugorje* (Hodder and Stoughton 1988)

Farrell, G. J., MM and Kosicki, G. W., CSB, *The Spirit and the Bride Say, 'Come!'* (AMI Press, Asbury, New Jersey 1981)

Hogan, F., *Words of Life from Exodus* (Collins Fount 1984)

John Paul II,
'For a Christian Europe' (Letter to the Presidents of the European Bishops' Conferences), *Briefing*, 16:2 (1986)
Redemptoris Mater, Encyclical Letter (1987)

Kraljevic, S., OFM, *The Apparitions of Our Lady of Medjugorje: an Historical Account with Interviews* (Franciscan Herald Press, Chicago 1984)

Laurentin, R. and Rupcic, L., *Is the Virgin Mary Appearing at Medjugorje?* (The Word Among Us Press, Washington 1984)

Laurentin, R., *La Prolongation des Apparitions de Medjugorje: Délai de miséricorde pour un monde en danger?* (OEIL, Paris 1986)

Laurentin, R. and Joyeux, H., *Scientific and Medical Studies on the Apparitions at Medjugorje* (Veritas, Dublin 1987)

'Lumen Gentium' (Dogmatic Constitution on the Church), in *The Documents of Vatican II* (Guild Press, New York 1966)

McKenna, B., OSC, *Miracles do Happen* (Pan Books 1987)

O'Carroll, M., CSSp, *Medjugorje: Facts, Documents, Theology* (Veritas, Dublin 1986)

Paul VI, *Marialis Cultus*, Encyclical Letter (1974)

113

Pervan, T., OFM, *Queen of Peace: Echo of the Eternal Word* (Franciscan University Press, Steubenville 1986)

Plunkett, D., *Secular and Spiritual Values: Grounds for Hope in Education* (Routledge, London 1990)

Rooney, L., SND and Faricy, R., SJ,
Mary, Queen of Peace: is the Mother of God Appearing in Medjugorje? (Fowler Wright Books, Leominster 1984)
Medjugorje Unfolds: Mary Speaks to the World (Fowler Wright Books, Leominster 1985)
Medjugorje Journal: Mary Speaks to the World (Fowler Wright Books, Leominster 1985)
Medjugorje Journal: Mary Speaks to the World (McCrimmon, Great Wakering, Essex 1987)

Tutto, G.,
Medjugorje: Our Lady's Parish (privately published 1985)
Medjugorje: School of Prayer (privately published 1986)

Vlasic, T., OFM,
Our Lady, Queen of Peace (a letter privately published by the late Peter Batty of St Leonards-on-Sea, 1984)
A Calling in the Marian Year (a letter privately published in Milan, 1988)

Works of prayer and meditation based on the Medjugorje messages

Medjugorje: Messages of Life (Dublin Medjugorje Centre 1988)

Barbaric, S., OFM, *Pray with the Heart: Medjugorje Manual of Prayer* (Parish Office, Blagaj, Yugoslavia 1988)

Vlasic, T., OFM and Barbaric, S., OFM,
Open Your Hearts to Mary, Queen of Peace, 1985 (the 'grey book')
Abandon Yourselves Totally to Me, 1985 (the 'blue book')
Pray with Your Heart, 1986 (the 'red book'), all privately published in Milan

Magazines published about Medjugorje in Britain and Ireland

Medjugorje Herald, monthly (Galway Advertiser, Church Lane, Galway, Ireland)

Medjugorje Messenger, quarterly (Medjugorje Centre, PO Box 702, London SW7 5RE)

MIR, monthly (Manchester Medjugorje Centre, 5 Oaklands Drive, Manchester M25 5LJ)

114

Printed in the United States
by Baker & Taylor Publisher Services